Tales and Flukes
from

Life in the Trees

Fractal One
Saving the Cosmos 'til Tuesday

Jim Loomis

Copyright © 2012 by James Cook Loomis

All rights reserved, including the right of reproduction in whole or in part in any form whatsoever without prior written permission of the author or publisher.

Copyright © 2010 Aquabet font

Published by:
Zantar Publishing LLC
Haiku, Maui, HI 96708

Design and Production: Barbara Wood

Jim and Barbara

Cover painting, "Life in the Trees" by John Severson
Watercolor, "United Species" by Danya Pharisien
Painting "Enchantment" (Jim as Wizard Merlin) by Andrew Annenberg
Earth from space, "The Blue Marble," NASA Goddard Space Flight
       Center 2002

Photo Credits: Alyssa Burtt, Valerie Kausen, Patrick McFeeley,
       Daniel McCulloch, Mike Neal, John Perry,
       Todd Swan, Rick Williams, Debbie Zarate

Library of Congress Cataloging-in-Publication Data has been
       applied for.

ISBN 978-1-62050-328-7

Printed in HK

Contents

Preface v

Prelude to Maui

Storm Love 2
Searchlight 6
Superman's Cape Foments Ape's Capers 10
Going Up 16
Carrots Called 24
Ambergris Adventuring 28
Zammy-fication 34
Some Boys Are Islands 40
Once 44
Phoenix, Icarus & FLO 48
Retooling Thoreau's Toolbox 54
The Mean Streaks of Bowl-choker Bay 60
Nevermore 66
Conditional Love 72

Poems

Popcorn 92
Beluga Wails 96
Aerial Crossroads 100
Stream Walk to Sea 104
Dolphin Mind 112
Laird's Big Blue Ride 116
Big Strapping Wave's Snapping Jaws Strapped 120

Photos

About the Photos 123
"Itta Bitta Zammy" 128
Elizabeth 129
School Days 130
Rowing Life 131

Photos (continued)

Teacher to Wizard 133
Off the Ground 134
FLO Saves the Whales 135
Cetacean Love 137
Extreme Life 138
Under Water 139
Making Her-story 141
Pirates, Ships, and Fish Tales .142
Stream Life 143
About the Photos (continued) .144

Maui

Uke China 150
Pliny's Revenge: Geometry 201 158
Indulgenous 166
Homo bogus bogus 174
Dr. Tabbo 178
PS, My Downfall 184
"ET" Mates the Great White Hunter 192
Sharkbite 198
Glaucoma 206
My Stolen Car 210
Whose Fangs? 214
Owning Things 220
Catmando 224
Pet Scan Ten? Nein, Eleven 230
Too Much Love, Too Little Violence? 240
More Than I Needed to Know I Learned in the Sandbox .246
Wandering Eye Takes "Hal" Out of the Loop 254
Blackwater 262
Archer and Lockyer 266
Ad for US (United Species) 274
Life in the Trees 278

Acknowledgments 283

Preface

Jim Loomis & daughter Megan Powers

Did you love the book, or maybe the movie, *Swiss Family Robinson*? I did. As a child it stirred in my little bones an excitement for living in nature up in the trees. When my parents moved the family to Maui in 1970, I was eager for the adventures ahead. We were like an "American Family Loomis." I guess as a four-year-old I had not yet become accustomed or attached to the form that houses were supposed to have. So when our house was a tent or a lean-to, a treehouse or a boat ... I was just wide-eyed and ready for fun.

The move to Maui was about living according to our ideals. It was about finding a way to live in harmony with nature, not against it, a hands-on exploration into living self-sufficiently. Maui made living outdoors a lot easier because there was no reason to fear freezing, poisonous insects, snakes, or mountain lions. When we weren't on the land, we were in the ocean skindiving, frolicking with dolphins, and observing whales. When we became aware of the threat to the cetaceans' survival, Dad joined a group of activists and traveled the world to help stop their slaughter. He also led rallies and protests against nuclear power and the testing that creates radioactive pollution.

Built into our daily lives were activities that kept our bodies healthy and strong, from carrying a five-gallon jug of fresh spring water up a steep, slippery trail to the reaching, pulling, ducking, and bending that came with growing gardens and maintaining the jungle that Jim had created. And all on depleted pineapple lands, I must add. Although living remotely, Dad always kept up with the latest scientific discoveries and with the state of our environment on a global scale. We lived outside of society, but he stayed current with world events. From the perspective of being on the outside looking in, he could see that modern civilization cannot sustain its current path. He has been a "scout" on the outside, living well, and here is the report of his findings.

Wanting to share his insights and inspirations, Dad began to write in the sixties ... and write ... and write ... and write. So now, five laptops and nearly fifty years later, he has a whopping smorgasbord of ideas, observations, and funny stories to share. A sudden change of fortune brought three generations of our family together for the past three years under one roof, where we have been working together to bring his books to the public. Consider this book an appetizer, a sampling of the many thoughts and stories his amazing life has cooked up. Savor these flavors and share them with your friends.

Megan Loomis Powers
February 2012

To the dolphins and whales — our water kin — whose joyful completeness inspires humanity.

And to my family: your love inspires my completeness.

by Danya Pharisien

"Slip into hammock … Enjoy long view …"
— Jim Loomis

Prelude to Maui

The schooner *Westward* c. 1910

" ... learn something about everything and everything about something."

— Thomas Henry Huxley

Storm Love

Kids have love affairs. Hard to say where they start. Mine were storms at sea, ocean storms. "Gale," "hurricane," and "typhoon" were my favorite words. The shapes of huge waves and the shapes of ships that survived them were my nature study. I saw every picture in every book in all the libraries in Long Beach, California, showing photographs of ships and storm waves. You saw aircraft carriers with their flight decks peeled back like sardine-can lids. You saw tankers with their decks so full of white water no one on deck could survive. And you'd see pictures of people crowded into a lifeboat that had survived after their ship went down. Big ships survived. Small ships survived. Mediums had more trouble.

"Why is that?" I'd asked my dad.

"How hard can you hit a feather?" he'd asked back.

That one got me into hitting feathers and watching birds. And that led to watching a friend hit a bird with a BB gun and watching it die. Knew I didn't want none of that!

But back to hitting feathers. Never could see how you'd ever hurt a falling feather hitting it with your fist. Dad had something there! And I could punch my fist right through a wooden orange crate. But not a cardboard box. And the bedroom door ruined my hand for a week.

"This is it," I told my dad. "If you're not strong enough to take a big punch, be light and flexible."

"If you want to survive," Dad added.

Joseph Loomis, my dad, and
WWII Japanese Zero fighter plane

"You can bomb the world to pieces, but you can't bomb it into peace."

— Michael Franti

Searchlight

A kid's early influences shape him. Our town was attacked by Japan when I was six. They shelled our oil refineries from a submarine. And tried to blow up our city's huge storage tank of gas. My dad was a meter reader for the gas company. There wouldn't have been anything to read if they'd hit that baby. Our town would have been burnt toast.

The skies at night would be streaked with searchlights, and air raid sirens would be screaming. My dad ran the big searchlight at the corner of our block. Our own planes would fly over at night, and the searchlight aimers would practice. Then the planes would speed up! My dad got pretty good. If a Japanese plane had made the mistake of flying over, the machine gunners and my dad would have made it their last flight. I hoped their plane wouldn't fall on us. Or on my treehouse in our back yard.

But I didn't just get to stand and watch. Not at all! I was six! I had to run down the block and knock on every door with a light on and say, "Lights off." Didn't want to be a target!

Once, I ran back to my Dad with his big searchlight blazing away at some aircraft streaking by overhead and said, "Lights off."

He pulled out a cigar, fired it up, and said, "Lights on." That's my dad. If you were gonna blast him to kingdom come, he was going to have a cigar or pipe clenched in his teeth. Rules were for other folks.

He'd shelled the Germans with a huge cannon in France in 1918. Twenty-five years later he was fighting them again. Germany and Japan had teamed up against us. My great granddad on Mom's side was a German. Taught philosophy at Leipzig, she said, wherever that was. Dad didn't seem to hold it against me. But he turned the big light on me twice, and I skedaddled.

Us *was* the USA. In my six-year-old mind, "U" and "S" were doing overtime in that last sentence. One big family: Us! No wonder those other guys lost! It took many more wars–some with US not winning–to get that we're all *us*.

"Courage is the first of human qualities because it is the quality that guarantees the others."

– Aristotle

Superman's Cape Foments Ape's Capers!

My bike was once my life and my delight. I made my money on it slinging papers, and everywhere was close with my speeding wheels. And getting there was great, especially to the beach. Only one way to carry a towel: tied at the neck like Superman's cape. Any old towel transformed you to Superman and off you flew, the towel whipping straight out backward in the wind from the knot of corners tied at your throat. I always knew that's how Superman would do it if just a kid again.

Capes gave a flying urgency to things it'd be tough to live without. Good deeds needing doing were got to best by flying capes, especially if it were a wet cape needing drying. (Superman could've took in laundry for a living if heroes got downsized.)

Beaches were the best excuse for capes. And a flying cape felt like you were on the way to saving something great. Maybe Lois Lane trapped in a burning building, or the Lone Ranger in a showdown he'd surely lose without you. My super-cape and I saved time spent playing at places other than the beach.

So with super-cape tied at my neck, I sped through a mile of parks to that golden summer beach. Rode past five little all-lawn curving parks and three big square blocks of parks with spreading shady trees, parks all the way. Full speed ahead ... flap flap flap flap flap! Magical Parky Place!

And when you got to the big street, Ocean Boulevard, where all the traffic was, there was a long down-ramp tunnel at *the end* of Cherry Avenue. You went down on your bike through the tunnel and turned right, then went under the busy street and under the very last park on the bluff and came out into the sunlight onto a big platform overlooking the beach. There was a long bicycle rack where you could leave your bike: never had to lock it. A set of stairs led to the beach, and big restrooms were at the bottom at sand level. And a big play-all-day sand volleyball court where you could make Superman saves and not skin your elbows. And then way out on the wide beach by the ocean was the three-story lifeguard house where they kept *the* most beautiful dory.

Through one of my dad's many miracles, I became a junior lifeguard and got to keep my little eight-foot foldboat right beside the eighteen-foot dory. I set floats for fishing and cooked fish lunches for the lifeguards so they wouldn't have to stop watching the beach for rescues.

I found most of the lost kids so the lifeguards could stay watching. If I didn't have a super-cape on when the loss was announced, I did when I started my search. I was a good "little kid retriever" because I recently had been a kid and knew pretty much where they'd go. Down wind was a good bet: kids don't like sand in their faces. I had to keep my super-cape out straight even running downwind, so I had to become a champion runner to do it. Running was great! Later, I'd run around the block every hour when studying all night for finals.

But back to lost kids. Where would *I* go to get lost? I'd look for some big attraction: volleyball, or big umbrellas, or a flock of seagulls arguing about something on the sand, or a couple of big pelicans, or people gathering around something strange, like a fish that came in on a wave, or maybe ambergris ... which was a prize I sought.

I never didn't bring back the kids. To see the tear-streaked faces of the moms and dads, having imagined the worst, instantly turning into the most relieved and loving smiles was my pay. I never took rewards ... just part of being Super-cape-man.

There was a hamburger and soda pop joint just off the sand that paid two cents for recovered pop bottles that made me rich enough to buy a hamburger for lunch. Then I'd buy a fudgesicle at another place for the bike ride home through the traffic-less curving parks. There weren't many cars. And not a lot of bikes either. Like a dream it was ... even then in '43.

(Drying my towel or playing Superman with towel capes came a long way flapping in the wind to "Saving the Whales" at the International Whaling Commission conference in '79, and then to the Millennium Edition of *Who's Who in the World* that covered my capers, like the virtual "*United Species 2000 Honoring All Species Underwater Parade*" with one hundred ninety-four flying capes of animals and nations. My bike and beach towel cape conspired to drive me to this book of apish capers. And if you look back, close and kind, perhaps you'll find in the archives of your mind your towels flying, too.)

"Don't cry because it's over. Smile because it happened."

– Dr. Seuss

Going Up

But me and my many kinds of homemade gliders–solid balsa wood and covered strut balsa and paper ones, and finding the right kind of weights to add and where to place them and where to grab and the right angle to throw them into the wind–is another story.

As kids, flying things always grabbed our attention. So I had to have a little funeral for the dead sparrow bird my BB buddy blasted. Kept her nice tail feathers. Buried her, and while her kids were cheeping, "Come home Mom with a worm!" from a high nest ... I was crying. Sad. No mom. Worm's turn.

Shocking!

But I dropped some worms in their nest for a coupla weeks with a can on the end of a bamboo pole, and things quieted down. Later, I'm sure I saw some small bird fly away.

Well, I plucked the longest feather from sparrow's tail and taped it onto my best glider. Called it "Sparrow" and drew a head like hers on it. Strapped Sparrow on my bike handlebars and pedaled her downtown to one of the tallest buildings. Mom and Dad worked there: I'd phoned I was coming. Said they'd come up with me on their lunch hour for the launch.

Elevator guys had got used to me by then. Winked and opened the "Keep Out" door to the roof, and Mom and Dad and I poured through it.

I was really excited 'cause the wind was out of the east off shore, a Santa Ana day. Leaves were blowing everywhere, even up the side of the building and over the roof.

Sparrow had been a big piece of slick, stiff paper from the corner store trashcan. I'd been saving it for a big event. This was it! Just great! Yellow. Big wind and a big slick bright yellow glider! I had folded the old news–"grapefruits five cents"–into the inside, written the *new* news–"Sparrow"– on both sides of the nose, scotch-taped that pretty black and brown feather on the tail, sketched her head and her bright black eye on there, and now she was ready to go. Mom had the six paper clips I'd asked for, and on they went by Sparrow's throat.

As the leaves were blowing up the building, I pushed Sparrow up and out into the rising wind and watched it shoot up past the roof on the windy side. We wowed as that Sparrow got up about a hundred feet and headed out past the building over to the beach. It was great! Doing just what you'd want it to do. Sail up and get smaller and smaller and disappear out over the sand and the sea. Wow! It did it. Then Sparrow even caught an updraft. Thermaling!

Mom and Dad were standing there flabbergasted by such a great flight. "Whee," Mom yelled and spun in circles, hands raised, her skirt swirling.

"Wow," Dad gasped, and took off his hat and scratched his head.

"Me, too," and I glided around the rooftop, arms outstretched like a bird.

"You know," Mom said, "a feather is a letter from a bird."

"Airmail letter," Dad chuckled.

"Saying what?" I asked.

Mom squinted into the sunlight looking for that gone glider and smiled. "Remember me, even when I'm gone," she said quietly.

I felt around for Sparrow's other tail feathers in my jacket pocket. "Well, if a living bird's a batch of undelivered letters, then what am I?" I asked.

"Same thing, but I guess right now you're a bunch of *un*delivered letters, to be delivered as you go along."

"Oh yeah?" I said. "Letters to who?"

Now she had me. "To God," she said.

"Unlikely," I said.

"You know, to the Cosmos," Dad intervened.

"How do you know?" I asked.

" 'Cause you're a *good* kid," Mom said.

We looked out past the sand to the sea searching for Sparrow. "Maybe I shoulda put pontoons on it to float if it reached the water," I thought out loud. "What about boats versus gliders?" I said to Dad, thinking of the pontoons I could have made and of Sparrow setting down on the water like a seabird. "Boats can float when there isn't wind and air currents to hold them up." I guess I felt sad. Yeah, sad.

"Wind and water are a lot alike," Dad said. "Two oceans, air and sea ... one floating on the other ... and both floating on the Earth."

"And don't forget those Great Edges in between," Mom said, "where one meets the other, where we happen to be." (They always did this, bring my attention to something bigger, loftier, more vast, when I got disappointed.)

"Yeah," I said loudly, gulping down my feelings and

chapter four, going up • life in the trees

playing along with them: "Air and Water Edge for Sailing, and Water and Land Edge for Surfing! Great Edges!"

"And every reason to *maximize* edge," said Dad.

"Why's that?" I asked just to hear what he'd say.

"You know, because that's where the *magic* is!" I knew there was more to this, Man being the magic-maker and all, but Dad went on.

"Did you know there are two more oceans? The Earth is actually formed of huge plates of cooled rock floating on molten rock floating on hot molten iron at the middle."

"Well, how 'bout that … four oceans," Mom said, "iron, rock, water, and air, going from down to up. And each is gliding on the one beneath it, and here we are standing on a pin-head of a building at the windy top." She brought us back to here and now.

"Yeah, but right now let's stick to water and air," I said, not liking the idea of what I was standing on being some kind of huge glider riding on hot lava down there right now one mile past my feet and gliding who knows where. But Dad went on.

"Earthquakes happen to be those plates rubbing, one diving under the other."

"Whoa …" I started flapping my wings in case we were

on the one going under.

"We're on the one going up," Mom said, and she snuck one last look out to sea for any sign of that Sparrow. "But in case we're not …" and Mom started flapping, too.

"I'm with you," Dad said, and he gave it his best flap.

(I think my recalling this story was inspired by daughter Megan telling me to give it my best flap as we dove through the backs of breaking waves and found ourselves in space with outstretched flapping arms falling onto the water.

"Give it your best flap, Dad!")

"If you have a garden and a library, you have everything you need."

– Cicero

Carrots Called

I'm grateful for the typing course I took sixty years ago. And agriculture: my carrot won first prize. Wish I had known then, that was the apex of my career. Apex of a water chimp's career. Not seaweed, but a carrot, orangeness bursting from the brown soil.

Mr. Moore taught agriculture. I memorized sixty names of plants and their shapes and sizes. *Pittosporum tobiras.* The name still resonates six decades later. It was to the left of the lettuce and crowded up against a fence. All sixty plants grew there in a small plot in the middle of town where we walked from our eighth grade classroom. Valuable local knowledge for the homeless–not a lot of those, then–or for hungry young athletes.

Typing and agriculture. Hoes and shovels to catch and mix the soil, typewriters to catch and mix the worded soil of culture. Later, a book I wrote won first prize on a distant island. That award almost matched the prize for best carrot, almost.

My school taught me high jump, shot put, broad jump–both standing and running–and then I won first prize in the pentathalon. And I won the fifty and hundred, which my dad had timed me on a hundred times between the telephone poles of our street. I still miss his raised arm, the bang, the smell of burnt caps when I got there. He let me subtract from my time the time it took for the sound to reach me. I told him I watched his finger pull the trigger, was going when the sound got there, though I hadn't moved: he let me subtract the transit time of light.

School did what it could for me. I liked it. Always wanted more. And got it. Now school runs a distant twelfth. Life changes. School taught me about that, too. Daily we changed into gym shorts and swung on what we could, lacking vines, as our latent chimp genes urged us to do.

I got to where the vines festoon every upright thing. Lots of vines. Which way to swing? Same as always: to a fun place to land, and a good time going. The book and green jungles of Maui were my carrot. I came when they called.

"... live your own life and live up to your own expectations."

— Tiger Woods

Ambergris Adventuring

Ambergris was what me and the whalers had in common. It was a treasure we both sought. Ambergris. Nice word. It sounded more romantic than it was. Ambergris is the last sperm whale turd one month into a six month fast. Crushed fermented cuttlefish bones.*

It was the world's most expensive perfume base. A million beautiful girls dabbed its molecules onto sniffable zones. Ears, too! Who would have guessed, a cuttlefish ending up so far from home. My last turd four days into a ten-day fast is a doozy. No market for *that* perfume.

When I was a kid, a big hunk of what I was sure was ambergris washed up on the beach. I thought I was rich. Hamburgers forever! I put it in a box, dragged it across the sand, wrestled it up the stairs to my bike, lashed it to the handlebars with seaweed, and pedaled home with the prize.

I yelled to Dad in the house that we were rich and come out and see why. He came out smoking his pipe and smiling

---

* In fact, ambergris has two ways to exit the whale, as barf or as poop. And, the longer it stays in the sea the more "precious" it becomes.

like "it was about time." He looked at it a while and named it "a gelatinous silver mass." That's what my dad called it. A gelatinous silver mass. He didn't call it ambergris.

"Are you sure it isn't ambergris?"

"Yep," Dad said. "Not a whale turd. A tanker turd. They wash out the holds of oil tankers into the sea about ten miles out, and we get stuck with weird petroleum glop on the beach. Tanker turd's what it is."

I liked "gelatinous silver mass" better than "weird petroleum glop," so I thought I'd quit pushing for ambergris before it got worse.

"Interturdal tank gloop," he said. He poked it with a stick, and it jiggled.

I got to thinking ... if folks thought those big, rough-looking, ship-sinking sperm whales made good perfume, what could the prettiest whale of them all do? Belugas look the way perfume smells. Stop you cold. Turn your head right around. Really pretty. And you should see their flukes! Belugas' flukes have these thin white up and down rear edges like a line of pelicans soaring up and down along the wave tops. Belugas are these Arctic white guys with bulging, quivering foreheads and the greatest smiles. They hang out around icebergs.

"Canaries of the Sea," they call them. Whistling like birds with turds smelling like perfume. That's some great whale!

Beluga ambergris–if they made it–would be a perfume treasure worth a fortune. As long as girls were girls and liked smelling sweet. And if you could find it. Since belugas didn't use toilets, it was out there in the ocean somewhere for sure. But then, even if you get the thing outta the sea... then what? Who buys it? But I guess you'd find out *who* once you got it.

So I further reasoned: the ocean was big and a tough place to look for things that were lost. Ocean being six miles deep, near frozen at the bottom, and storms tossing on top– with sharks, eels, killer whales, drunken speedboat drivers, moody whalers, and the like–you might wish you'd just swung by Longs Drug and picked up a dab of "White Shoulders" for the girls (Mom loved it!) and skipped ocean adventuring.

But then having said it, I knew it was totally wrong. So I turned tail and declared out loud, "Everything but ocean adventuring is henceforth a crime!"

That rang kinda hollow, though ... too harsh or something. How about change *crime* to *pastime*? But then, that didn't sound right either for worse reasons, because adventuring with vines and pools and waterfalls and with all the *land* critters was good adventuring, too. Tarzan would agree.

So *land* snuck in with *water,* and I was trying to exclude *air* to give my program a little definition. But the program wasn't goin' for it when I got to thinking of the nifty birds like those sunrise, chirp-singing cardinals and nighttime owls, and how I liked my gliders so much. So I just let *air* in, too–with breathing and all. But I knew I had some good, strange momentum going, so I drew a big line in the dust with my toe and stepped up to it with total resolve and said it: "ADVENTURING, ambergris or no ambergris!"

No question though that this ambergris perfume would be big in my life somehow: I knew it. *Beachcombers' blessing.* That *thing* came in on a wave when I was watching. Meant for me. I saw the whole thing. First I saw it in the wave's green breaking curl with light shining through, and it was looking really out of place.

And to me, this whole adventure meant that *I* was *out of place* in cities. I wasn't going to have to go to work in cities to live. Belugas didn't. Tarzan didn't. Treasure would ride in on a wave to me. Some great sea thing would come to me if I was ready. I vowed to be ready.

That's what I was telling myself when I pedaled it home: if this ain't ambergris, it's a spy, and it'll tell me where the *real one* is. So when my dad poked that "gelatinous mass" and it jiggled, my brain jiggled, too somehow. I spoke right through that imposter to the *Real One:* "I'm ready: find me!"

Johannes Brahms at the piano, c. 1889

"Quality time spent with children could earn you immortality."

– Lehua Loomis

Zammy–Fication

"Zammy" is a word I have never seen 'til just now when I typed it. Yet it must be somehow strangely unexamined in my mind, for my most cherished–and now remembered nickname–always used for me by my super Uncle Joe was: "Ittabitta Zammy." What might he have seen in me to call me such? Zammy = Zany? Shazam = Zammy? Ittabitta Zammy = a little bit of zany Captain Marvel magic?

Uncle Joe and I lived only one mile from each other in Long Beach, California, so to ride my bike that quick mile to his house seemed so right. Together, we'd take the short walk to the wide, long beach. Spending time with him seemed to say that a lot of what you most want was best. It seemed to say that a little effort can get you a lot in life, and the *right kind of a lot* was important. What we both seemed to want most was a swim together–and a run and catch a few waves and get back for a little sit-around-talk or a new movie by the kids. And we'll have some popcorn before dinner, during and after. Why not? Stuff you most want to do was to be done.

But he might have been teaching me some sly code, like: life's a movie, always. So popcorn is always appropriate. Who knows? Too late to ask.

The judge, Uncle Joe, lived three blocks from the beach. His house and yard took up the whole end of the block. Must have been two lots. His wife, Helen, was my grandfather's sister. And *her* sister, Aunt Alice, who always lived close, was another of those famous Indiana Thoma sisters, all come to meet their men and birth their babes in the golden "Sunshine State" back in the thirties.

Uncle Joe's kids, James and Joseph, were early artist intellectuals who made eight mm movies so frightening that I'd choke on my popcorn. They would make movies of chessboards with self-moving pieces and perhaps a snakelike scarf moving through, by shooting one frame at a time. Early set-piece animators they were. Their movies always had strangely unusual visuals and mind-stretching titles, like "Transfiguration" and "The Ghoul's Blood".

And they even animated entire piano concertos, with each musical phrase a new visual situation. Then in a black, lightless room, with a fragrant bowl of hot popcorn, the opening scene of the movie would be accompanied by

James's crashing piano chords in total darkness–his piano at the other end of the room fighting for its life as he attacked in a Brahms concerto kind of mood.

A picture of Brahms was on the wall by the keyboard, and even I noticed that theirs was the same looking piano–with wildly carved legs–that Brahms was pictured playing.

The word genius was never misused in describing the boys. Later, James set scholastic records at Stanford, and then Joseph came along and broke them.

Joe Maltby, their dad, the Superior Court Judge, was my uncle and swimming cohort. While his kids made films, practiced piano, wrote poems, and devised elaborate ways to confuse Joe's ninety-year-old dad, living in an attached dwelling, Joe and I would swim to the next lifeguard tower and run back. You felt great! Then walk home.

Uncle Joe taught a men's Bible class at the Grace Methodist Church where I was baptized and where Mom played organ. Later, I helped make our church the league champion year after year by pitching strikeouts and hitting home runs with my mom cheering in a red hat.

I can't recall what Uncle Joe and I talked about when walking to and from the beach more than sixty years ago. I wish I could. I bet it'd tell me why he called me "Ittabitta

Zammy."

I don't remember when or how he died.

But I know I really loved him then–and now–for taking me to run and swim with him. And I feel I keep his love alive by naming fish and cats funny names with kids and swimming and running and rowing with them.

"… paved Paradise and put up a parking lot."
– Joni Mitchell

Some Boys Are Islands

As a boy with a rowboat, my playground was a group of low sand islands in Alamitos Bay. One side of the bay was Long Beach and the other side was Seal Beach–so named because seals sprawled themselves all over the little sand islands and produced a chorus of barking–and Long Beach, because of the long, wide, white sand strand facing the open blue Pacific. Both were tourist attractions and beautiful, un-crowded places to live. The seals agreed and flourished.

What could possibly threaten such natural beauty?

Oil Money! It destroyed them both before my bewildered eyes. The names of two cities, their whole *personas*, made obsolete! Seal-less Beach and Long oil-derricked Beach staggered on, steel shadows of their former selves. Or Seal Beach, because an *oil seal* must have busted on an oil derrick offshore. That could account for the black surf ... and the black goop between your toes.

Oil was discovered off the coast of Long Beach, so the

city went into the oil business. That meant phony islands with oil-derricks, made to look like apartment buildings littered the water between the shore and breakwater, being miles of piles of huge boulders that finally grew as long as the beach itself. Then, since no surf could get to the beach to clean its white sand, as it had done twice a day for millennia, huge, noisy sand-cleaning machines had to chug along at night to do the job, needing bright blinding lights to see their way, all on the energy of–you guessed it–oil. And then, no one was allowed on the beach at night: might get in the way of the machines.

So with all that oil money, the city surely needed some yachts to spend it on. And you can't have your yachts running aground ... so the little sand islands were dredged from Alamitos Bay to create a yacht harbor. With the islands gone the seals had no home and disappeared.

And why not a new yacht club? Strange fluke that the man who built the Long Beach Yacht Club and was elected commodore years later became my father-in-law. His daughter was the best thing going.

But when I think back to my painful childhood stammering, I wonder if that trauma wasn't caused by Seal-less Beach, and Long-gone Beach. What is a kid to believe ...

when well-loved islands disappear and towns' names are ignored?

Imagine yourself standing alone outside on a starry night looking at the moon ... and all of a sudden ... the Earth disappears from beneath your feet! Looking down ... stars below! Yikes! Foundation gone. Maybe my *speech foundation* went out with the islands.

John Donne's poetic statement, "No man is an island," missed the point. "No man should be an island *remover,*" should've been a commandment. Confused baby seal crawls up on me for a little nap while I'm floating around out there where the islands used to be, I'll say, "Relax, baby seal, all aboard, this *boy* is your island for now. Fergit Donne."

Once

Career preference tests in high school
Showed my clear interest in being a
Lighthouse keeper.

I was tall like a lighthouse:
I had lenses at the top like a lighthouse,
My mind felt like a penetrating beacon,
Lighthouses stood where the shore meets the sea,
my usual habitat.

You were a guard for others,
Lonely civic duty:
A lifeguard in a lonely lighthouse,
Lots of time to read.

Storms were what had put you there:
And fog. Shining through the fog,
Shining out to sea in a black and roaring storm,

Lighting the way for others ...

to miss the hidden rocks,

to find shelter in the hidden lee.

Being an unknown,

Keeper of the light,

Saving lives with light

When they feel most close to lost and lightless

black.

A *tall* lighthouse anchored on lonely, rugged

land-sea edge,

Or on a sturdy lightship far from land,

Caught in the same black maelstrom,

And shining, facing the towering seas.

I was a natural:

Never wanted any other,

Would rather help than gather wealth,

Once I grasped that Life was Once.

"It is easy to make a buck. It's a lot tougher to make a difference."

– Tom Brokaw

Phoenix, Icarus & Flo

Living only one house from Lockyer's Market and being honest, I got hired young and did everything you can in a store: checker, shelf-stacker, vegetables, deli, and meat. I take that back. A nice Chinese man named Paul did vegetables. I just sprayed them with cold water.

Later, I even caught most of the fish they ordered for the market. It was a standing joke: I could fill their orders in my fourteen-foot fishing boat with its twelve-horse-power motor at Horse Shoe kelp, six miles off the coast. I just trolled with feathers or baited hooks from the bait boats or fished the bottom for what was wanted. Easy. Fish rather than fisherman were in the majority then. You just went to where they were.

But first, I proved myself as the ash man. They had a brick fireplace outside, and I burned most of the boxes and shoveled the ashes into the left-over boxes. And then the trashman took them. The tall chimney would be shooting sparks, and ashes were flying.

It might have looked like I was just shoving cardboard past that steel swinging door into the roaring fire, but if you looked into my mind you'd see I was stoking that fire fierce to keep the bad guys from catching up. Or, we were setting some speed record, like I was doing a *John Henry* shoveling sixteen tons of coal into our steam engine racing against some new-fangled big diesel train one track over.

Fifty years later, a book I wrote won first prize at a writers conference, and the featured speaker said something ridiculous, like: "There is only *one* story being told."

Right! Oh, yeah? What?

"Phoenix* rising from the ashes," he said. "Everybody crashes, and if you're still here, it's because you figured out how to rise from your ashes. You're glad, and you're telling your story, leaving your map."

So then, of course, the first thing you do when you get your groove back and dust off the ashes is get fitted for some new wax wings and try to fly to the sun. But Icarus's wings melted and he fell into the sea. So there I was, stoking the furnace of the speeding launch to save Icarus before he sank. You can't keep a good bird down or let a good birdman drown!

* Eygptian mythology: large bird in the desert consumed self by fire, then rose living from its own ashes.

The book that won is a true story that includes some global eco-caper prankster adventures meant to:
- Save the Whales
- Save the Dolphins
- Save All Life (anti-plutonium)
- Save Man from himself
- Save the Earth from Man, and... well...
- *Save the Cosmos ('til Tuesday)*, by Bong Quixote.

Your normal six pak. (But there's a mysterious seventh can in the middle ... shhh ... stay tuned! That's another story.)

First on the list, Saving the Whales, required a one hundred ten foot propane fired hot-air balloon, a smiling whale called, "FLO" (Flying Leviathan Object). A sea mammal sculptor, John Perry, designed her because he was determined to resist the extinction of whales and dolphins. John formed a group of thirteen, known as the Whale Nuts, and led our efforts to Save the Whales in America with a full film crew.

I rode in a bamboo basket a few feet beneath a circular propane burner attached *to* and hanging down *from* the middle of FLO; but the massive smiling whale had a nasty habit of prefering to turn over, belly up. And me now upside down within the basket and on top of the propane burners??? And a hundred feet in the air?!

Uh oh, the Hindenburg revisited. (At least my ashes wouldn't have been crushed badly by a falling piano. And what was the Hindenburg's piano player doing *not* wearing a parachute anyway? Or *me*?)

Well, as a matter of fact, this is what was *projected* to happen if we hadn't re-designed the bridle and propane lines on FLO which managed to keep her belly down. Her smiling, upward curving head and upward curving tail with her downward belly had created *two* places for the hot air to rise. She was a whale with more than one upside, but that had created instabilities.

Her technology revised, FLO presented an unforgettable smiling whale for all the world to see, making showcase appearances in the U.S., England, Denmark, France, Japan, and finally at the International Whaling Commission meeting in London. We had gathered activists from all over Europe and Japan to push for changing the reality of whaling practices. These practices were thought of as "gentlemanly" divisions among certain countries allowing for the horrific murder of ten thousand sentient beings a year. With thousands of youthful FLOing activists staying up all night chanting in five languages my compilation of one hundred reasons not to kill whales, the doors burst open at five in the morning and the word came: a million square miles of the Indian Ocean were now safe for sperm whales, and commercial whaling had been called off for ten years to let the whale populations rebound.*

Longtime "insiders" said that nothing like this had ever happened before. FLO, a huge airborne smiling Whale, rather than morbid pictures of dead and dying whales, gave the commissioners something happy to indentify with, and had been the crux of the change. Following the announcement, we Whale Nuts were honored at a celebration dinner hosted by ten conservation groups in attendance, as having "Saved the Whales." We had at last flown–like Icarus–to the sun, and the whales had risen–like the phoenix–from their own ashes.

---

* There's still much to be done for whales and their kin, the dolphins. It wasn't until 2009 that the Academy Award winning documentary *The Cove* exposed for the general public the slaughter of dolphins at Japan's Iki Island, acts we had hoped to stop in 1978. At this writing little has changed

"I went to the woods because I wished to live deliberately, to face only the essential facts of life and see what they have to teach, and not come in my later years to realize I had not lived: living is so dear …"

– Henry David Thoreau

Retooling Thoreau's Toolbox

By age eighteen I had read all of Thoreau* and was impressed by the quality and simplicity of his observations. He was having a better time on the Concord and Merrimac Rivers than I was with my beach-and-bike and the entire Pacific Ocean! Or at least it seemed like from the quality of his insights.

In one account he imagines his neighbor, a farmer, coming down the road toward him with his mule and tools and family and forty acres on his back. Acres were ache-ers: oh, his aching back! So Ole Henry imagined how satisfied he himself would be just to drill a few holes for air in a six-foot toolbox and move in.

I did take part of his advice and ignored the rest. Forgot my tools, left them out in the rain: that way they couldn't trick me into becoming a slave to them. Seemed the same as being a servant of your talents, instead of *them* serving *you* appropriately.

* Henry David Thoreau, 1817-1862, American essayist and poet.

And I upgraded the toolbox considerably. Forget the holes: make one big hole and leave off the roof. The whole thing made for fresh air and the sky above. And why a rectangular tool box, when it could be a curvaceous rowboat? Make your toolbox your tool! So at eighteen, I did, and moved in.

Why *not* live in your rowboat tool? Where everything likes rain and water, and rust isn't a problem? Oarlocks are made of brass, so that takes care of that. And the wood of the boat and oars thrive on water: it's what grew them. They feel right at home in a good rain or storm! And it gives rust that sleep* it's been needing!

My good mechanic friends had all given away their tools after they found themselves in continual service to their friend's broken-down cars, and made to feel responsible if the one fix didn't last forever, or was followed by something *else* going out. They would be somehow responsible for a *lifetime* for their friends' junkers, and there were a lot of them. Toodeloo tools! Splash! Good riddance.

Of course the toolbox-rowboat being the tool, and a beautiful and useful one, had a huge payoff! Almost as big a payoff as moving from a home to a mansion. Who could

---

*"Rust never sleeps," an old adage of mechanics and such.

sleep in a regular bed in a roofed house when you could be rocking in the sea looking at the stars? Silly! Grownups? "Groandowns," I called them.

The sea was always called the Mother, but it was a little tough to figure out why, until you felt how thoroughly she rocked you. It put you kind of at the infant stage, which should help with not growing up too quickly. It had nothing to do with *infantry*, unless war is our infant stage, which it probably is.

Sure, I slept summer after summer in my huge beautiful rocking toolbox, but that wasn't the half of it. My boating buddy, Ben, and I rowed to islands and around them, camping everywhere. We rowed to where the fish and lobsters were, and the dolphins and sharks and whales. Blue sharks were everywhere in those days. I'd see twenty, just rowing to Catalina. "Beautiful Blues" that didn't attack you over nothing, flashing around you even when you were swimming and diving deep with the dolphins.

When the hammerheads made an appearance though, I hightailed it right back into my toolbox. Their eyes sticking way out to the side like that looked too weird, and they had gotten a bad reputation for their occasional bad behavior. But I think they were overrated for badness, or you wouldn't be reading this. 'Cause I've seen them move so fast that I could never have made it back to the comforts of my toolbox if I was seriously on the menu! But now, there is a lot less *menu* left for those big eaters, so these days the "men" in "menu" might be you.

But other stuff you could do with your boat was all that stuff I did, summer after summer, like girls and diving and dolphins and abalone and watching swordfish sleeping at the surface. And getting to row anywhere to see anyone at any time who was living on a boat for the weekend or for life. And those were pretty often folks I naturally liked a lot, 'cause we had the love of the sea in common.

Broke my heart years later when Natalie Wood drowned in Emerald Bay on Catalina Island. She would have joined me on a row immediately, given the chance. Dumb drunks on big yachts were the only bummer, and you just rowed away from those lost souls.

So I never aspired to a big house because my rowboat was already so much huger than a toolbox. And then many years later in Hawaii, when I came to build my six-year-old "pirate" grandson his own pirate ship in a tree that had the dimensions of half of the great cabin of a major sailing ship, like Captain Cook's, or the same amount of room as a modern million dollar yacht, it was pretty easy to imagine ourselves as secret millionaires, dressing down. I'd invested in a strong rower's body and Speedos™ with my millions.

Of course, if you live in a dirty, crowded, and cramped human city, you could see how the race was on to get a big air-conditioned penthouse. *More* might be better there, but in Hawaii, *less* most always is. Nature is so huge and beautiful, and warm outside. That's how the Hawaiians used to do it! Made little houses, but they were out the door into huge beautiful nature before the sun came up, to say good-bye to the stars. How *little* can you put between you and Nature is the question here. Why have a "six mil" roof when a "three mil"* roof will do? A house costing over a buck is an unnecessary extravagance!

Then I thought about my mentor, Ole Henry, no toolbox or rowboat. Maybe he was just aspiring to be comfortable in a coffin, accepting the inevitable. That's where he's been spending his time lately. I'm next, and I'll have had some practice, too.

* millimeter, as in thickness of plastic

The seven masted schooner *Thomas Lawson*
New Bedford, c. 1902-07

"There is nothing in a caterpillar that tells you it's going to be a butterfly."

— R. Buckminster Fuller

The Mean Streaks of Bowl-choker Bay

Rocking gently in my little boat on a quiet morning, I laughed to recall that other morning when this impressive anchorage had been christened Bowl-choker Bay. It became so named in the summer of 1957. My dearest and funniest Catalina beach-bum rowboat buddy, Ben Floggins, had taken a weekend job as a deckhand and guard on a yacht that had positioned itself next to my bobbing rowboat home. Dressed in a white yachting uniform bearing the yacht's proud name in gold and with tasseled shoulders, Ben alone guarded the home grounds while the owners proceeded to the Isthmus Restaurant for breakfast. Alas, as it turned out, his time would have been better spent guarding the home *waters*.

Last night's dinner clamored for release from my morning bowels, and having no bowl but a large bay, the very Isthmus Bay upon which my boat floated, said bay was selected as the recipient of the used food that had traditionally assumed a tubular and yacht-like format. Today was no exception … in format. But length!?! Destiny called!

Having launched this uncommonly monstrous tubulosity (UMT) at the extreme depths of my early morning dive, the fish and I had ample time to regard this spectacle as it slowly floated up, but with a clear sense of purpose and direction, towards me! I hastened to my boat above and scrambled in … and with a growing sense of alarm!

I watched with amazement, as UMT unfolded its destiny. Having been launched at the depths of said morning dive, rather than sink or be torn to shreds as usual by a dozen fish who now hovered wide-eyed watching the proceedings in amazement, UMT attained the surface, fairly breaching like a whale. It then proceeded to follow me back to my rowboat, bobbed close at hand, and waited.

"Bowl-choker!!!" Ben gasped, astounded.

I watched. It waited. I watched. It waited. I watched; Ben watched; the fish watched. It waited.

Finally the silence was broken.

"Rig me," it said.

"Dig me?" I asked, seeking clarification.

"Rig me," it repeated–in no uncertain terms.

My mind swam in disbelief … Dig? … Dig into dirt and be buried rather than have a free life on the open seas?

Cat turds, maybe! Dolphins', never! Yet mine ...?

But right there in front of me was this handful of party favors, toothpicks with colored rectangular paper on the top. I had wondered earlier why my rowboat had come to be the way-station for these leftovers from the big oceanfront dinner bash birthday party for which I had played ukulele and been given access to the immense quantities of food which had now been miraculously transformed to the UMT that bobbed patiently at my vessel's side.

"Rig me!" I heard repeated with growing impatience.

Boom! Aha!! My mind exploded in illumination, glistened, then contracted into total clarity, as I did God's work, that only the humble are chosen for, and rigged eight toothpick-masts with colored sails along the handsome deck of UMT, thereby exceeding the previous record of seven masts on the historical gaff-rigged *Thomas Lawson* out of New Bedford.

In proud parental joy I saw UMT maturely leave the protection of my vessel's side. It then proceeded swiftly and directly towards Ben's excellent craft.

Ben's laughter turned to concern and then panic, as said vessel lay over in the wind handsomely, filled its sails with a CRACK like the best Lipton Cup challenger, and chose a course amid wind and wave directly toward the mid-section of the gleaming yacht whose defense fell solely upon the broad shoulders of Ben.

Ben responsibly snapped to attention in the best tradition of a slave's defense of a master's possessions and disappeared below. In but a moment he re-appeared armed with a long aluminum boat hook to fend off the incoming torpedo in the best of maritime martial-arts maneuvering.

 Alas, the lengthy tube and the yacht's high sides made it an unequal match. What thrusts of his, intended to disrupt the attack, were easily dodged and ultimately unsuccessful.

UMT plunged to its mark against the yacht's sleek sides on the crest of a large wave leaving a long and unmistakable signature. Sweat beaded Ben's brow as he observed in the distance the yacht's owners returning from breakfast in their launch. UMT slid-sailed down the length of their boat, came about smartly, and charging through the waves bashed into my boat, losing a few masts, and then sailed out of sight into the open sea.

Upwind! Square-riggers don't do that!

Ben, the fish, and I immediately calculated the odds of these things happening so perfectly and concluded, correctly, I believe, that God not only *does* have a sense of humor, may have *missed* the "little sailboat phase" as a kid, but would surely *spare no end* in humiliating us for any temporary diversions that would take us away from rowboats to yachts, away from naturalness to fanciness.

"Thus Spake Through-a-Turdstra," said Ben.

That seemed to sum it up!

"It's not that I'm afraid to die, I just don't want to be there when it happens."

– Woody Allen

Nevermore

When I was a kid, I discovered it was often easier to just do what Mom said than go into oppose mode. As long as your mom has a good flow, why vote no? Left more time for "YES fun" and didn't waste time on "un-fun NO". She made a good home for me and had a lot more experience. So when she rarely said, "Just do it!" ... I just did.

Now Mom Earth has an old-time good flow going. Been nurturing and protecting life for about four billion years. That's why you're here. So when she says, "Die," I'll just do that, too!

You could see every living thing would someday not be. Time was running out for us all. The whole *living now* slate would be swept clean in a hundred years. And piled full of new guys and gals. So you could get with the program or oppose.

You see your cats and dogs and painted turtles getting stiff and disappearing. You see your friends and granddads gone. Something serious going on. And the whole trend says, "You, too!" And you don't like it.

"Nevermore" is a tough word. We flee. No wonder. To us, *thinking* (alive) sounds better than *not being able to think* (dead). 'Course if you're in big pain, *not feeling* sounds better than *feeling.* But in general, thinking has got some kind of fulltime upper hand on feeling–you never want *not* to be able to do it. "Nevermore" is a thinking man's word, as Poe's raven would have us ponder. But it has a most unusual feel that you can learn to like.

My cat, "Gee Willoccurs", flees from surprising new things. Then he comes back and sniffs them. Coupla re-sniffs and he settles down and gets even with a few fleas. "Even" is about the best you can hope for with fleas. Poison 'em and you end up poisoning you and the cat, too. Cure worse than the curse.

Yeah, us humans got a surprising new thing, too. Not the *act* of Death, but the *fact* of Death. Go ahead, flee again, then come back and sniff the thing, and see if it's all that bad. Yeah, I know it's sad. We woke up and heard, "Good-bye." Shocking. So we've got this *flee*-bite of Death to deal with.

(Gee Willoccurs's fleas aren't *all* bad, anyway. Makes him stretch every which way and lick and do a lot of flea bite-cat tooth coordination that could come in handy. Or pawsy. Yeah, that's better, Fleas Pawsy, that's what Willoccurs's got!)

Well, if you ask me, Mom Earth has a pretty solid case for *us* going with *Her* flow. We're the new kids on the block. And She never even had blocks before. Something curious right there. Any being in for the long haul would go for a re-sniff on blocks! But then, we're told, "Curiosity killed the cat," so there are tough calls, no doubt!

But being "curious" could lead to changing a course that might *need* changing. You know, what's even *more* curious is to keep going the way we're headed, toward extinction. We've received an invitation to join the dinosaurs. You think some future life form'll use *our* bones for oil to drive on Mother Earth or Mars? Not likely. Party's over, if we don't get a true foundation for Global Civilization. For now, we've got all these myth-maker guys growling at each other and waving their Big Bombs.

So I say, go with Mom's program and learn what MOM is, rather than buy into the myths Man sells. Learn about both, if you have time. But start with truth. Stretch your mind and scratch: learning *what is* can save us.

What is is Mom's language, called Science–*knowing*. It just could save us from that far distant unavoidable extinction–our sun's Earth-scorching Red Giant phase. That is, if we can just get past Man's "weapons-gone-mad" phase that threatens an avoidable extinction from a thousand little suns made ready to explode over Earth's cities.

    Well that's about it for MOM Ed 101. And my mom added as she said good-bye, "Go out there. Enjoy yourself! Have a good time!!" And she had a good time saying it. Goodbye wasn't bad. Just inevitable: unless "science-gone-mad" has its way and puts an end to dying. If it does make us immortal, it better make us small. And if it does, watch out for Gee Willoccurs!

> "Anything worth doing surely is worth doing badly."
>
> – E. K. Chesterton

Conditional Love

"On one condition!" Her flashing eyes pierced my brain. I reeled, never having been seen so deeply. "On one condition!" she demanded. "On the condition that you will never, ever, not once say to me, 'Mother, why didn't you make me continue taking piano lessons?'" She meant it. I never said it.

Twenty years passed. I never touched a piano. To me, pianos symbolized the killing of my mother's dream. Her dream had been a good one, and I had always liked it. Still do. She, my sister, and I would be a musical trio on steamship vacation tours, live adventuresome lives, see the world, get paid for it, enjoy what we were doing, happy, together. Happy together.

I wished that there were two of me. One of me should have done that, wanted to. Trouble was, the body I was in–sitting on that piano bench with her–gazed passed the tiny, black, crammed musical notation on the sheet music, out the window to the big open baseball diamond across the street, ringed in palms and bathed in light. Over there, in that golden childhood setting I was the sixth grade Adonis hero–fastest runner, nearly unhittable pitcher, and the homerun king.

    Daily I reveled in my pitcher's windup, then explosive spiral unwinding, and release of a perfect pitch. I thrilled at the "whump" of my bat sending the ball over the fence where balls were not meant to go and had never gone before–through the mayor's windshield for one.

    Not only was I the longest ball hitter that school had ever seen, I was often totally confident of where I was going to hit and would call it beforehand.

    "Deep left field," or "half way up right field fence."

    "What you going to hit next?" a gang of admirers asked one day.

    "Dog," I said. It just came out like that.

    At that moment I had noticed an old dog being walked by an older man beyond the fence across the street, an outlandish and impossible shot. No ballistic trajectory, not even in curved space could connect ball and dog. Trees, phone lines, electric poles, cars, fences, palm trees–everything was in the way. The dog never knew what hit him. Neither did the old man who found himself towing him, dead weight on the quiet end of a short leash.

"Wizard," people said.

"You brute!" said others, mainly girls.

"Shot the ole' codger in the dog." All true, I guess, but I secretly wondered if the dog wasn't perhaps a suicide case and had used me.

Windows and dogs, knowing they were fair game, came to avoid the area. When my homerun ball knocked a pelican out of the air, the school principal showed up to take away my bat. I surrendered it willingly. Pulling a loose two-by-four out of the backstop, I hit a homerun with bases loaded. I couldn't be stopped. Winning streak. Everybody knew it.

I also pitched like a fiend. The connection of muscles in my long arms and broad shoulders gave rare leverage, and I broke old tossing records all through school. Even to get the bat in the way of my fastball was to risk having it broken. I dared bats to get in the way. My fast curve balls were positively going after those bats. They rarely met. No-hitters were common.

Those were realms of pleasure wherein a sixth grader could abide. And those were things I was doing *then* rather than practicing for *later*. And even the word "practicing": it felt that if you gave up the present moment for another time you could get lost. Right over there, right now, was the beckoning baseball diamond, where a game would assemble if I arrived. I didn't want to be on the bench for anything, not now or ever, piano bench included. And wasn't this what God wanted for us, to enjoy the world? Right now? I surrendered to baseball.

So Mom delivered her brain-searing speech, and I made my way, dazed but off the bench, to my oiled leather trapper's mitt, ball and bat and was soon running in the sun, friends gathering. Mom's and my one lifetime conflict was over in seconds. We spent our remaining years enjoying each other.

In the great Piano vs. Baseball War of '46, piano lost, but hadn't been shut out. It got a point. Score: Piano 1, Baseball 1001. After two weeks of lessons I had played a simple song quite well for my sixth grade class. No question that I was talented, liked the piano, loved my mother, wanted to play that part in her dream. My eighth grade sister played her part by playing the cello. With Mom as violinist, I was definitely the missing piano in her steamship dreams.

And I knew that not to play the part (only I could play) in a grand dream of the one-and-only lifetime of my only loving mother conferred special demands. I had to weave some equally beautiful dream of my own into the fabric of existence. I didn't know what dream, but I knew I'd know it when I saw it. It didn't help that my sister became a good cellist.

It did help that I became a great baseball-ist. Year after year I pitched and hit our church team into the championships. Mom, Elizabeth, was my best fan, never missing a game, cheering like mad in a red hat as I fanned their best man or sent the ball flying far over the fence.

But Elizabeth's dream of being free to sail and play the waters of the world with her musical children was canceled. She smiled, settled in, and laughed away her life doing a million other worldly things. Mainly, in her spare time she played organ. This part of her dream was her reality. Elizabeth had graduated from Oberlin College in music and physics with a specialty in pipe organ. She had even played violin in the campus string quartet. As an organ student, she had the distinct honor of sitting on the bench next to Rachmaninoff as he played. Holding my growing hands in hers, she told me his were twice as big as hers.

After marriage and children she played organ every week in a church. I say *a* church, rather than naming any church because she played in many churches, the ones where the organs were best. Her religion was the organ and the great organ pieces, mainly by J.S. Bach. When she played her sermons in pipe-organ-Bach, the pastor had a tough act to follow.

So she played her organ, and I pitched my curves. She supported my baseball. I supported her music. How did I support her music? Every Thursday night I guarded her at church from nine at night to one in the morning, while she practiced organ for the coming Sunday church service. Guarding was made necessary by the little-known history of foul deeds practiced upon organists by late night lunatics. Such warnings came in organists' journals, she said. Or maybe she just tricked me into soaking up a thousand hours of great organ music. For my part, getting soaked in sound like that wasn't a chore. Anyway, I was the protector but not the pianist.

As protector, hundreds of times I lay on wooden pews with Bibles or hymnals for pillows, looking upward at elaborately carved columns, casements, and stained glass windows as she immersed both us and the huge stone church in the great and thundering organ music of the centuries.

It was there I learned that I had a special love for the *Toccata and Fugue in D minor* by Johann Sebastian Bach. It thrilled me deeply, and once I had requested a midnight replay and gotten it.

Looking at the vaulted, soaring ceiling of that old stone church, I supposed it was the architect's fancy to make room for God, and perhaps room for Man to hold such elevating thoughts. But the music couldn't be contained. My mother's musical/mathematical mind and heart brought to many a quiet, black night a cosmic message to awakening worlds. The stained glass windows, vibrating to the organ's thundering tones, transmuted sound to light and conveyed the wave lengths of Bach's music out through the night sky, past stars, and outwards toward galactic brightnesses. I fancied this as Earth's harmony with the music of the spheres and a grand "hello" to any other listening ears.

The years passed. My parents had divorced two years after my birth. You wouldn't have known it. Joseph, my father, was ensconced in my mother's big reclining chair just about every day, cigar in the ashtray, when I came home from school. He said he was cogitating. It was what I called snoring. He worked as a gas and water meter reader and was often home by noon. When he awoke we were both ready to discuss that month's *Scientific American*. He owned every issue.

Joseph built telescopes, ground his own lenses, looked at the stars, wondered, announced each pinprick of indistinguishable light with a history of the star or galaxy or nebula's composition, mass, size, and age. That was good. This was better: if the fish were biting, he composed notes to the school administrators describing the condition forcing me to lie abed. The truant officer wasn't fooled. After Dad donated one of his telescopes to the school, the notes got simpler: "Took Jim fishing." Times were easy.

Although my sister and I lived with my mother, and my father occupied a small room a mile away most of his life, family projects were many and successful. Nearly every evening started with a three-hour-long dinner where philosophy and laughter were ever-present. No family arguments arose in our twenty-six years together. If voices were raised, it was in song.

The years seemed to pass in quiet perfection, and all the various maturity hurdles of the fifties I duly jumped– degrees, work, marriage, cars, homes, children, taxes, insurance. As Zorba observed, "the full catastrophe." Baseball gave way to everything. My tools of play were disassembled.

But not my mother's. During the war years, Elizabeth roller-skated the four miles back and forth to work at the municipal courts when the bus drivers went on strike. Skating either way, she would gather about a hundred pigeons that awaited the toasted breadcrumbs she prepared every morning. On certain weekends when the dandelions were first blooming, we'd awaken at dawn and together raid the neighbors' lawns for the yellow buds to make dandelion wine.

Elizabeth never stopped playing.

No sense of expectation or disappointment ever arose after the accepted condition of never asking her why she hadn't forced me to continue taking piano. My mother, who had indeed been filled with expectations for her son's musicality, seemed not to have learned the bitterness of expectations unfulfilled. She never again expressed any hope for my life career other than perhaps, "Go out there, learn, enjoy, have a good time." I suppose it was inevitable that the relentless perfecting quality of the universe toward Love would eventually dispel any family disharmony from my not playing the piano.

GRANDDAUGHTER

One night in April years later, I phoned Elizabeth after midnight to announce the birth of a daughter, Megan. It was spring vacation for me, a high school mathematics teacher with a week off. Mother remarked that she had just that morning played my old favorite, the Bach *Toccata and Fugue in D minor*, for the Easter sunrise service at church. Fifteen years had passed since she had given me that midnight re-play of it, and I asked if she would play it for me now if I drove the twenty miles down to the church.

"Gladly," she replied.

We met outside the church at two in the morning on a clear and windy night. The moon was full, splashing light on everything. I had asked some question as we walked down the stone path to the huge wooden doors. I realized that Mom wasn't talking or answering any question as she unlocked and swung open the vault like door. I laid her sleeping grandson–my first-born four-year-old, Gannon–on a pew, and then we proceeded in silence to the organist's loft. She pointed, still not speaking, to a small recessed ring in the ceiling and indicated that I was to pull it. From the roof a stepladder descended, unfolding itself, and she motioned that I climb the ladder. Once in the room above, I realized that the immense bass and middle range pipes of the organ were there. Then she motioned me further upwards to climb a second ladder leaning on the pipes themselves. I climbed that ladder and at her further mute directions, crawled over, and sprawled on the organ pipe openings themselves. Then, she disappeared.

A minute of silence passed before the opening line of the great toccata blasted my body and ears like a hurricane. This is the piece James Mason, as Captain Nemo, plays in that brooding last scene in the movie *Twenty Thousand Leagues Under the Sea*. The deep organ tones rose, shaking my body and inhibitions loose. As the music gathered momentum I heard someone's paean of joyful screaming and crying and laughing intermingled with the massive fugal structure. My own. Our three souls soared I know not where. The Witness was demolished. A giant cry of joy and pain, of humanness and super-humanness rode the night wind.

The sound's great power and elaborate structure tore to shreds any resistance, and after the composition's awesome climax I found myself lying clean and purged and exhausted on the pipes. I climbed down and hugged my mother. Tears streaked my face. Nothing was said. Words felt too puny. I drove home, son sleeping, his head on my lap. Visions heretofore unseen fluttered off their roost. What they were wasn't clear.

The following evening the new intimations crystallized. I had been playing a record of Beethoven's "Moonlight Sonata" for Gannon, telling him of this new life, a sister. She would be coming home from the hospital with Diana, his mom, the next day. We looked at the full moon and listened to the haunting, first movement. Reaching over in the dark to replay the record, I hit the needle arm causing a deep scratch across the whole section, ruining it. Gannon had fallen asleep, so I found myself going to the piano bench to see if Diana had the music for the piece. It was there, and for the next ten hours, until the sun rose again, I wrote the names of the keys on the keyboard, found a chart relating the keys to notation, and decoding, taught myself how to read the score. Remembering the sound of the melody and harmony, I played and memorized, line by line the opening page of the music.

I was shocked and thrilled that the beautiful music could flow through my fingers, that one could proceed with desire and get to exactly what it was one wanted to do, without a teacher or lessons or exercises. What was intimated the night before coalesced into the perfect plan to pay back my mother for the mind-blowing toccata Easter present she'd given me.

It was this: I would invite her, a year from then to the yearly pre-Easter talent assembly program at the high school where I taught mathematics. I would tell her to take the day off work and come up to hear a recital given by a mutual friend of ours, a classical pianist. What she wouldn't know– until the lights dimmed, the spotlight illuminated the school's new nine foot Steinway, and the tuxedoed pianist strode in lofting his tails over the bench as he settled at the keys–was that the pianist would be *me*. I would excuse myself to do "gate duty" a few crucial minutes before the opening, and in those moments the last pieces of the drama would be assembled.

I would teach myself piano for one year, taking no lessons, running no scales, attending no classes. I would pay her back, great friend that she was, in kind.

That year my next thought was always, "Where's the next piano?" Throughout the year my free periods were scheduled in whatever part of our school a piano was available. An enthralled, running, budding pianist found his way to one of those pianos daily.

We brought a piano that had been Diana's from her parents' home, replacing the little keyboard on which I'd started to teach myself. Late night playing competed with class preparation, but I managed.

By the year's end I had learned six pieces, three* being ready to perform. I had played each from beginning to end a hundred times. I had listened to good recordings of great pianists. I could relax and simply let the music pour through me. But looking at the keys became a positive distraction, looking at my hands, a disaster. This was tactile knowledge, finger knowledge, hand-arm kinesthetic knowledge, not sight or thought. Interrupted, I would have to start at the beginning of each of my three pieces. But uninterrupted they

* *Sonata in C# minor* (first movement) by Beethoven, *Prelude* in C *from the Well-Tempered Clavier* by J. S. Bach and *Prelude in C# minor* by Rachmaninoff chapter fourteen, conditional love   life in the trees

flowed like water.

I knew now why Elizabeth was so hurt by the early ending of my piano career. I had been missing a close and constant love. My musicality was, however, on thin ice, with this awkward inability to discover the musical path, once deflected. My prayer was that this fear would not be visited upon me in a critical moment.

My musical offering would consist of the three pieces, opening with the "Moonlight," then Bach's Prelude in C (upon which Gounod wrote his famous melody *Ave Maria*), and finishing with Rachmaninoff's grandiose *Prelude in C# minor,* the very piece Elizabeth had witnessed the composer himself play in concert in her college days. Mother and I had agreed that this was the piano counterpart in greatness to Bach's *Toccata and Fugue in D minor* for organ that I loved and had been loved by.

The day of the concert arrived. Elizabeth came early, and I showed her the newly built architectural showcase where the concert was to be given. It was a giant fluted parabolic auditorium seating fourteen hundred and was an advanced and exciting sculpture. A great cement arching backbone rose to meet twelve one-hundred-and-ten-foot-long fluted parabolic ribs. These concrete ribs were cast on the site, each then forming a pattern for the next, and lifted into place by a crane. The mathematics of its forms became part of all my classes as it rose outside the classroom window over a period of two years.

As Elizabeth grasped the beauty and economy of this new construction technique, I ushered her inside to the stage and to the great, black, gleaming concert Steinway. She played a few simple notes, letting them sustain long as the overtones ranged and mixed to silence. We sat together on the bench.

"Mom?"

"Don't say it."

"But I was a great baseball player, wasn't I?"

"Do you play anymore?"

"No, I guess I don't." (I hadn't played in fifteen years.)

"You could throw a great curve."

"That I could."

"Could you still throw a curve?"

"That I can and some new ones, too."

We smiled deeply into one another's eyes.

The bell rang for the assembly, and I took her to the best front-row seat. When over a thousand seats were filled with noisy students and their teachers, I excused myself according to plan for a few minutes of gate duty and then donned rented lace and tuxedo. I spied her looking for me as the principal finished his opening remarks, wondering why I hadn't returned.

    The thick red velour curtain slid back slowly. Lights dimmed. With my white lace shirt and black tailed tuxedo I was a good match for the gleaming jet black and ivory piano to which I confidently strode under the following spotlight.

    Settling onto the bench and beginning to collect myself, as I remembered having seen other pianists do, I found it impossible. Forces of dispersion were much stronger than those of cohesion. The sound pressure of fourteen hundred healthy high school kids who were now totally silent must have created a vacuum. I fell in. The enormity of what I had done by coming before this huge energetic, focused crowd, having had no previous performance experience, destroyed any last hope for control. As the quiet deepened, though not religious, I prayed. Light blinded. Time was melting. I had to start. As my hands lifted and began the descent to the keys, I noticed that they were shaking visibly and hard. There was too much energy to handle. Release was the only hope. I had one flashing remembrance of a quote that I liked, that helped make this possible, and chuckled a little which helped, as my fingers touched the keys, paused, and began unfolding the early undulations of the first movement of Beethoven's "Moonlight Sonata." That quote, one that has helped me a lot when embarking upon epic voyages that hold good chance of final flaws, is, "If a thing is worth doing, surely it is worth doing badly." Failure laughingly covered, I embarked upon success.

My fingers were trembling and sweating so that I abandoned myself even further in the face of these pressures and my inexperienced reactions. Winging it as usual but with an assist from my tail feathers hanging over the bench, I heard from some dreamlike place the great sonata pour forth with heart and hope, a gift in some Santa Clausian sense.

Everything flowed, not perfectly but definitely passable and surely surprising to my mother, at whom I glanced for the first time at the conclusion of the second piece, unable to risk it earlier. Elizabeth looked as I had felt, lying on the throbbing pipes of the great organ: glowing, joyful, exhausted, her face also streaked with tears.

Before the prelude by Rachmaninoff I quieted and began collecting myself for the sound assault of that song. She would know immediately from the first note the parallel of this piece to the Bach Toccata and Fugue, and that the origin of this musical flowering was the seed watered most crucially by her the previous Easter.

The dazzling, chiming prelude unfolded with its rising crescendos. The power built. The keyboard was awash with sweat. Coming off the powerful climax, my fingers slipped, splayed. Sweat seemed to explode from all my pores. A paralyzing fear was close. My fingers fought for their knowledge, their way, exorcising thought. Body/mind battle. Feel fought thought. Thought lost. The music didn't stop but did include a passage not written that rambled on for about five seconds, then returned to the theme, owing to a telepathic call to my mother for help. I whispered, "Thanks," as the thunderous piece quieted to silence.

The gift was delivered. I rose and the audience rose in ovation. My mother clapped and cried and laughed and shouted, "Bravo!" probably knowing "encore" might find me lacking, having given everything.

Poems

Popcorn

Shucked Himself: *The Perfect Ear*!

Of silks and leaves and perhaps a worm

'Til golden kernels popped full beautiful

From hot oiled Time's pan

To *Us's*–no *Thems*,

'Til a random funfull shuffling brought

Your *in*–my *out*:

Affinity's fit makes *We*, makes *Us*,

Makes *He, The Perfect Ear*,

Harder to find.

But there's *ME!*

Yeah, puffed up like mad,

But who remembers our

Golden-rowed Togetherness

Or ... at least likes the idea of

The Perfect Ear having laughingly forgot

How to unpop his parts.

"Squeaking my high notes"

Beluga Wails

Knew I's a Beluga since I's two–
Smile, upper lip, delighted roll up eyes–
Saw a pair in a pool at a zoo:
Looked just like me and
Squeakin' my itty-bitty high notes, too.

Wondering ... since a kid when first we met,
Old friends since first I saw them in
White ice, white snow, blue water
White tremulous foreheads, singing
High notes unknown 'til now,
Beyond the range of normal microphones.

Diving together,
Crystal clear beneath the bergs,
Frozen ice and freezing water,
Comfortable.

Polar bears were the problem:

Knockout blow and dragged on ice

When you surface for air,

Dinnertime for bear–

Isn't nice,

Isn't fair.

Not surprised to see as years roll by

I'm in a book with a cover of a lady

Smiling at my old friend, white Beluga,

Who's smiling back. (He'd whooshed her
> with a mouthful of water!)

Nor that the lady's husband,

Famed dolphin scientist, John Lilly,

Having heard of some "dolphin man",

(Being listed for fifteen years in a book* he wrote)

Walked a long and rugged path, 'though aged
> and frail,

To find me.

Programming and Meta-programming in the Human Bio-computer

He set about quizzing me and exclaimed,
"First man to pass all my tests!"
Then, swinging in my vine-wreathed couch
By waterfall, remarked, "Jim, I envy you!"

We speculated together, swinging there:
Our genes were mainly formed
By a million years of being prey.
New thing now, unique: a preyless predator–
No fear of tigers, boars or bears–
Having tools of sharpened mind.

Who else but Men so turned the tide,
Then called themselves divine?
Predation habits kill our kind:
The threat of "them, not us" remains.
Pre-emptive strike?!
Ruthless logic of the "if … then" mind, *
Isn't fair,
Isn't kind.

* Can Quantum Mechanics lead us to a humane logic of "both and more"?

Aerial Crossroads

Far from home and penniless,
Poised to leap off a sheer cliff,
I heard a voice speak from above,
"Better know what you're doing!"

A hang-glider shadow passed over:
"I do," I said,
To the marriage of wind and wing
And stepped off
        Into what has been death for many ...
But became soaring poetry of exultant heart,
As Rick with tandem hang-glider and I as passenger
    Caught the wind
        And stopped the upward rushing ground.

Wheeling like birds,
We joined hawks,
    Radio controlled gliders,

        Parasails,

            Solo hang-gliders,

               Paraplegic pilots rolled off cliffs by their friends,

And great V flights of pelicans touring the white surf
        far below.

Above swimmers, skimmers, windsurfers, runners, and
        surfers,

We joined the ancient field of soarers …

        Lofty Leonardo,

              Stratospheric Bach:

                      All those beings of winged mind

Peered through our eyes

        Down toward the cryptic code

        Evolving hologram of Earth.

Spiraling up and down,

We stitched together once again

That wedding of fear and trust

That weaves the world.

Dedicated to my second son, Rick Williams–explorer, adventurer, inventor, playful pray-er, prayerful player, cherished teacher–in great appreciation and respect.
                                                      Dec 16, 1989 - Zantar

Stream Walk to Sea

(To be read slowly)

In peaceful treehouse–morning thunder.
Huge waves strike high sea-cliffs throwing spume
    into sky.
Massive cliffs shudder in seaquake.
Wave-grooved bay beckons.

Swing down from treehouse, stretch, bow to sun,
Walk alone on the footpath towards the sea.
See what you see: Up ... Infinity; Down ... bright
green, deep-streamed river valley.

Feel the sun on your shoulders: feel the moving air
    on your face.
Listen to the sounds of birds and distant ocean
    waves.
Smell the seasoned earth where the flowers exude
    their fragrance.

Taste a hanging lilikoi: see what draws your gaze,
    nose, and tongue.

Walk with spine aligned, easy and erect.
Experiment with gait and breath to what feels most
    delicious.
Breathe your boundaries larger.

Drop thought, hopes, expectations: doing is done.
Feel free to *Be*.
Seek no memories: find - outside your mind.
There, the smell of coffee from Danya's house.

Take the path beneath the mangoes to the stream.
Morning light sparkles off laughing river.
Slip into the source of this humor. Laugh together.
Slip from pool to pool, being ancient water creature
'Til you come to high cliff edge over pool below.

Body rising, balance tall on back hooves,
Extending your seeing seaward.
Curl toes over rock at cliff edge.
Feel ancient earth beneath feet.

> Hologram you
>
> Give your body
>
> Back to God
>
> To BE through.

Leap into sky—enjoying gravity.

Feel the rush of wind and pure *support-less-ness.*

Pointed toes cleave water—

Feel upward rush of bubbles over body,
> an airwave massage.

Light above water shafts deep into opened eyes.

Effortlessly float upwards to surface,

Face parts silver dancing curtain, finding air.

Blow breath like whale in sky;

Watch rainbow mist drift by mottled rock face.

Float with open eyes, head back, air-stretched chest
> lifting to heavens.

Watch quick insects dart above, under branches
> hanging over pool.

Listen to breathing: feel the body rise and sink
> with breath.

Reach for the clouds with your chest.
Inhale them. Swallow rainbows slowly.

Lift knees to chest rolling backward; hands reach
    out, body straightens.
Point toes to sky and unfold torso downward.
Let weight of un-buoyed legs shoot body-arrow
down, Earth-center-seeking.

Allow upward float, point toes to clouds.
Cross feet and wave "Hello" dolphin-style to clouds,
    bathing in light.
Backward arching, spiral and spin upward to air.
Move like a 'gator to pool-edge rocks.
Climb up and step from rock to rock downstream.
Listen to the click of bamboo in the wind.

Swim the long pool beneath the old abandoned mill.
Walk the sheer pool edge where the waterfall drops
    into the small room.
Sitting in stream, let the falling water rub last
    burdens from your shoulders
And wash residue of thought and time downstream.

Dive, arcing into the next pool, and swim around
> corner.

Look for frog beneath moss there by the cave.

Cross peninsula where old sign on tree says,
> "Dog Drowned Here In Storm."

Feel love of man for dog. Feel love of dog for man.

Feel love.

Love feel. Feel. Love.

Walk over vertical basalt rock hexagonal network in
> shadow.

Hold tree branch and swing around river-twist

To where streambed opens up to sea.

Look for ducks in bubble-cave, years gone wild.

Wild mallards now in residence. Quiet. Walk slowly.

Avoid the predator stare: dry your wings in sunlight,
> too.

Sheen of feathers–green and glowing blue in cave–

Make sky and grass colors pale.

Baby ducks walk from cave a hundred heartbeats
    later.
Rock ants stumble through leg hairs.
Butterfly watches from nose.
Dragonfly lays eggs in pool.
Fish catches mosquito. Crawfish duel in shadows.

Three leaves float together through air to surface,
Race off as runabouts, tumble over rapids into pool.
Downstream now, there, the river meets the sea,
Beyond the bubble-cave with goldfish in its pool.

Fresh stream water tumbles into salty ocean over
    slippery rocks.
Ocean surf splashes upstream to greet it.
Massive surf runs along black lava jetty.
Blue waves break white over outer bay reefs.

Stereophonic roar of big waves
Breaking around circle of bay at different times.
Seabirds float on wind, settle onto rocks and
    reef edge,
Careful to heed the wave's eviction call.

Sun slants rays deep into blue of bay.

Dolphins watch from neutral corners

As the sea once again assaults the land,

And the jet-skis race with tow-in strapped-on
    surfers

Far offshore at Jaws, three coves west.

From "Synchronicity" – "Yin and Yang" – photo by Daniel McCulloch

Dolphin Mind

You have never missed a sunrise on the ocean,
You have never missed a sunset on the sea,
Your life is a weaving through the interface of two
    oceans.
Far above the ocean-air the starry patterns wheel:
Only storms and sun hide stars.

Your moves are the motions of reproduction, a
    flowing undulation.
Your eyes see all around you at once, a three
    dimensional sphere.
Another seeing–a seeing of sound–senses and
    assembles
Three-dimensional pictures from sound
    in your mind.
You send these scenes whole as sources, bypassing
    linear language.

You have no walls or boundaries.

Food is plentiful–feeding is fun.

Dolphin friends follow and feast:

Your group mind grows and sings its learning.

You have no fear of falling,

Your pleasures are flying,

You wear no clothes,

Your body is too beautiful to hide.

You follow every breath you take,

You have always been awake,

One side of your brain sleeps at a time–

Circling, sleep-eye in, kids in the middle,

shark-watch-eye out.

You need nothing that isn't available–

Ubiquitous abundance,

Joyful completeness.

You think; therefore,

You think you'll play

All day, again today.

Laird's Big Blue Ride

Kapalua dolphin tribe
Feeling big north shore waves
Flees west shore trash.
Flukes fly low beneath blue giants' north shore roar:
Clean currents and trash-less sand
Look like seashore's face before
The era, water-ape, began.

Yet Laird's wild white thin signature,
Written quick against impending scatterment
Across encyclopedic sound,
Tickles dolphins' fancy,
And they rise to this occasion's roar
And watch the jet ski's airy trail–
Rope-shadow and skimming surf board
With Laird's upright shadow dancing–
And take new interest in these water-apes
Who rape the earth and run with wolves,

But still, like they, would ride the waves.

Laird is towed and whipped and thrown
High on the face and tickles the brow
Of a doomed, ungroomed and laughing Blue Giant,
Two weeks fresh from Alaskan storm.
Full of itself and quickly growing, Blue Giant trips
On Peahi's big wave-building reefs.

Trips on Lord Laird's land and lore,
On this north facing sun-swept shore.
Wild haired forlorn face reaches for Laird,
But too late: gets Laird's white thread
Wake of skipping water-sled instead,
And humps and throws and reaches
And must settle for man's screeeeeches!

Now begins the crash to the floor,
To the feet of the giant of land
Named for a God-man, Maui,
Who from a cloud on a cratered volcano
Lassoed the sun in its course.
Laird is flying low and is screaming,

His screams lost in the roooaar
Of the throes of the death of the Giant.

But his sea-written, white skimming trajectory isn't!
Lost in foam but caught in light on photographic film
By chopping copter's cockpit camera,
These pictures ride our minds in waves of
      consciousness–
We, these Blue Pearl tipping Terra riders.

This wild light wave
Caught in torques' orbits.
Elemental scene ...
      masked as mass
      marked as matter ...
LIFE–riding these steep galactic arms
When Blue Giant plummets to its doom:
Yes ... the hiss of falling foam
When Blue Pearl Planet Giantess
Is plunging to emerging Life.

Big Strapping Wave's Snapping Jaws Strapped

Thundering north shore Maui wave,
Dark foreboding nighttime thunder,
Sunlight reveals the size and source:
Thirty foot northwesterly,
Deep furrowed to horizon,
Strap-boards unstrapped, unsheathed
Towing jet-skis fueled
Gunned, launched and gone:
Word spreads, even to Jamaica.

Rastafaris liked the surfers' talk of Jaws,
Something their own Jah would do
Or have them do for fun:
"Jah would go," breaking no jaws.

Court no fear that Jaws break you!
The impact zone
Of curling wave-of-time is near,

And there is no escape!
Strap in and thrill to inhabit a position
So close to liquid catastrophe ...

And yet evade its curse,
Is to steal food calmly from the god of death,
And laughing, picnic smiling,
Eating slowly, sleeping quietly
In the light of breaking shade.

About the Photos

1 – "Itta Bitta Zammy"

    A & B "Getting into the swing of things"

    Taken a couple of years before helping my dad in "Searchlight," these pics are clearly a case for "Zammy-fication."

    C & D "Learning the ways of water with my big sister, Jo Anne"

    Here's proof of my being a budding gardener ("Carrots Called"). Jo is at the spigot, and then she is "watering" me! It worked: I grew.

    E   "Playing in the sand with Jo Anne and friends"

    Pre-kindergarten, we began to learn the teachings of "The Sandbox."

2 – Elizabeth

    A   "Elizabeth, my mom, in taffeta at her baby grand"

    At age sixteen, my mom was laying the groundwork for a lifetime of music. Seeing this photo, I get the importance to her of raising a musical family ("Conditional Love").

    B & C "High Fashion Model" – "Flapper? Yes sir, one of those…"

    She posed for these shots c. 1925, before marriage and children and the Great Depression. At this time she was also playing organ in silent movie houses. She told us that one night she fell off the bench laughing at Laurel and Hardy.

    D   "Young mother"

    She was the family photographer and rented an 8 mm camera once a year to document our changes and to show us the growing collection from the preceding years.

    E   "Me at eleven with my pal, Mom"

          This sunny So Cal day was sometime following "Storm Love", "Superman's Cape", "Going Up", "Carrots Called", "Ambergris Adventuring", and the beginning of "Conditional Love".

3 – School Days

    A   "At fifteen holding up my 'cheerleader' sister, Jo"

          She seemed light as a feather. These days are touched on in "Conditional Love" and "Archer and Lockyer".

    B   "Aboard my first house boat at the Isthmus on Catalina"

          That summer of 1955 I had in mind a "new kind of man" for myself, one who would be a troubadour with eight hours of poetry to share. It was then that I memorized one hundred poems and *The Prophet* by Khalil Gibran.

    C   "Ben"

          He was my best around-the-island rowing buddy for two long summers. This is the very Ben in "Re-tooling Thoreau's Toolbox", and "Bowl-choker Bay".

    D   "Bill Lockyer ready for the '32 Olympics"

          The city of Long Beach hosted the Olympics at its Marine Stadium that helped to set a standard for rowing there. It was at Lockyer's Market that I stoked the fire in "Phoenix, Icarus, and FLO." He helped me find the lapstrake double-ender in "Archer and Lockyer".

    E   "Coach Pete Archer" in "Archer and Lockyer"

          All agreed he was some coach! They named the rowing center after him. There's that grin.

F   "First crew team, Long Beach State College, 1958"

I'm the guy on the right ("Archer and Lockyer").

4 & 5 – Rowing Life

4 A   "At sea, alone together"

Article appeared in the Long Beach Press Telegram, August 1963. If you look closely you can see in the background the "Pike", Long Beach's famous fun zone, now long gone, with its "Cyclone Racer" roller coaster.

B   "Fifteen foot fiberglass row boat"

Its experimental design made it fast, light and unsinkable.

C   "Stand-up rowing (SUR) my twelve foot wooden lapstrake with wine glass stern"

In Alamitos Bay, Spring 1955, I took a break from finals at Long Beach City College. This boat sat upside down atop my Nash (that I could sleep in) throughout my college years. This followed the time of "Some Boys Are Islands".

D   "My fifteen foot Spruce lapstrake double-ender"

At Emerald Bay, Catalina, Summer 1963. With oar extensions and sliding seats, this is the boat Diana and I rowed the channel in.

5 E   "The Family at Emerald Bay, Catalina, 1968"

Here we are: Gannon, soon to be eight; Diana; "Dory", our noble friend; Megan, age two; and me with our fourteen foot Coast Guard cutter lifeboat, *Serena*.

F "A row along the Lahaina coast in *Volup-scrumptious Pie*"– Spring 1976

"The happiest day of my life," Meg had said, as we sailed home at sunset, oars for mast and rudder and towels for sails. Ian Mac Intyre is in the bow.

G "More 'mucking about in little boats' " *(Wind in the Willows)*

Megan and her kids, Zen and Shakeena, practiced their strokes in Maliko Bay, Maui, in *Rowmance,* 2011. This and *Volup-scrumptious Pie* were both cast from the mold of *Serena* but with an added two feet of stern extension, keeping the same length at the water line. Sheer beauty!

H "Hauling out at Makena Landing, 2010"

Rowmance appeared in Maui's own movie, *Get a Job.* She was lampooned: it was funny.

6 – Teacher to Wizard

Mathematics Teacher (c.1962) to World Activist to Bong Quixote to Wizard - around the circle of painting (I posed for the wizard.), "Enchantment", by Andrew Annenberg

7 – Off the Ground

A "Contemplating"

The silence and weightless, peaceful feeling that happens right after leaving the ground is in stark contrast to the tension, clatter of gear, and heavy foreboding that precedes jumping off a cliff with a hang glider. Landing in a hammock can provide a similar contrast. Ahhh …

B "Gliding over the California coast at sunset"

The glider flew from Mt. Tamalpais and over Stinson Beach.

C	"Pilot Rick Williams dangling upside down from glider, waving streamers"
D	"Occupy Hammocks!"

Best with uke and boogie board strategically placed to cushion the falls.

8 & 9 – FLO Saves the Whales!

(All here as described in "Phoenix, Icarus, and FLO.")

8 A & B "FLO (Floating Leviathan Object) at the Statue of Liberty"

That's me swinging in the basket beneath the burners next to Liberty.

C	"Moving fast to light the fire under FLO in front of the White House"
D	"FLO beside the Washington Monument"

This was a great caper! In the view of President Jimmy Carter and Japanese President Ohira–after the smoke cleared from the twenty-one Gun Salute–there floated FLO for all to see. Save Those Whales Now!

9 E	"FLO beneath Tower Bridge, the Thames River, London"
F	"Big FLO at the Eiffel Tower"
G	"Leading the 'Sanctuary for Whales Parade' with uke at Whaler's Village, Maui"
H	"LIFE Magazine Article, June 1979" At the Capitol and Mt. Fuji

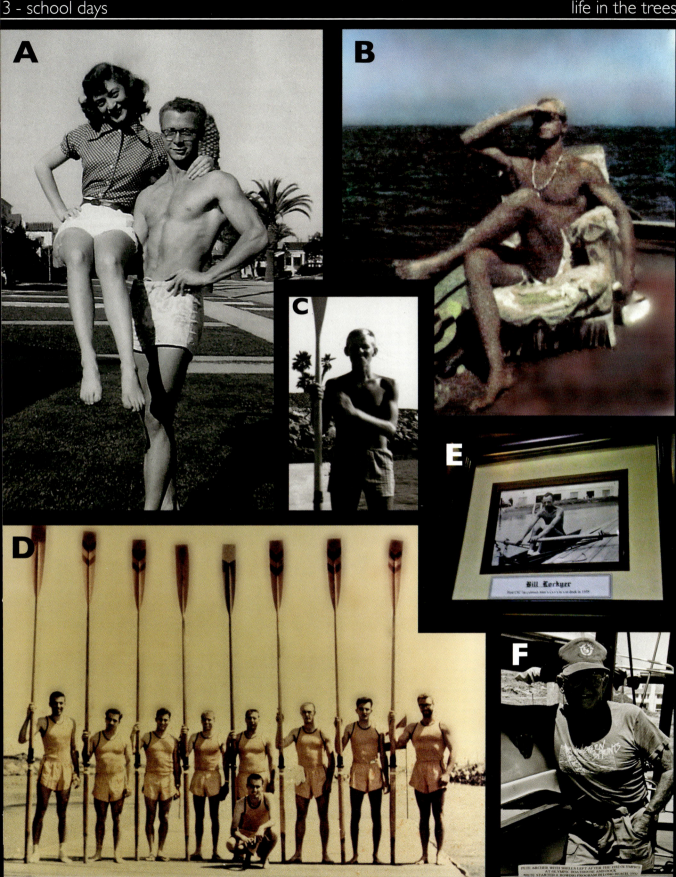

AFTER GRUELING CHANNEL TRIP, L. B. SKYLINE GREETS COUPLE

Man, Wife Row Channel

By GEORGE ROBESON

A young schoolteacher and his wife Friday rowed a 15-foot skiff from Santa Catalina Island to Long Beach in hopes of reviving the channel-rowing competitions of years ago.

James C. Loomis, 26, former Long Beach State College mathematics instructor, and his pretty 25-year-old wife, Diana, shoved away from the island shoreline at 10 a.m. Friday and pulled into a dock near the Reef Restaurant at 3:30 p.m., after five and one-half hours of pulling the double set of oars on the little boat.

"It was a pretty uneventful trip," said Loomis, who will begin teaching high school this semester. "The water was pretty calm. We went through a school of small whales once, but they did not bother us."

Loomis said his wife, a former drama major at LBSC who played the lead in several college productions, "did a little better than half of the rowing."

The couple and their baby son have been spending the summer on a houseboat at Catalina, but intend to move to the Redondo Beach area. Their problem: who will tow the houseboat across the channel for them.

It's too big to row, even with the lovely Mrs. Loomis doing more than half the work.

Shown above in Malibou Lake resident Jim Loomis who recently rowed his skiff alone from the mainland to Catalina in 5 hours, 19 minutes, one of the fastest times ever recorded. Loomis hopes to row to Hawaii in 1969. Loomis says rowing alone in the sea makes you become aware of your place in the universe. A lot of people need that.

5 - rowing life

life in the trees

6 - teacher to wizard · life in the trees

A

B

D

C

7 - off the ground
life in the trees

Big Protester Stages a Float-in

LIFE June 1979 Volume 2, Number 6

Flo, a 110-foot inflatable whale, is traveling the world over to dramatize the plight of her kind: the whale population is shrinking, mostly as a result of Japanese and Russian slaughter. Flo's sojourn is sponsored by her creator, John Perry, and a coalition of conservationists seeking a moratorium on commercial whaling. She visited the Capitol *(upper left)* to inspire legislators to put economic and diplomatic pressure on Japan and was an uninvited guest when Prime Minister Masayoshi Ohira visited the White House. When the International Whaling Commission, which sets kill quotas, met in London last year, Flo kept vigil *(upper right)*. She has also floated for freedom past the Statue of Liberty and made a pilgrimage to Mount Fuji *(lower right)* as an appeal to the commission, which meets in July to decide the whales' fate.

10 - cetacean love life in the trees

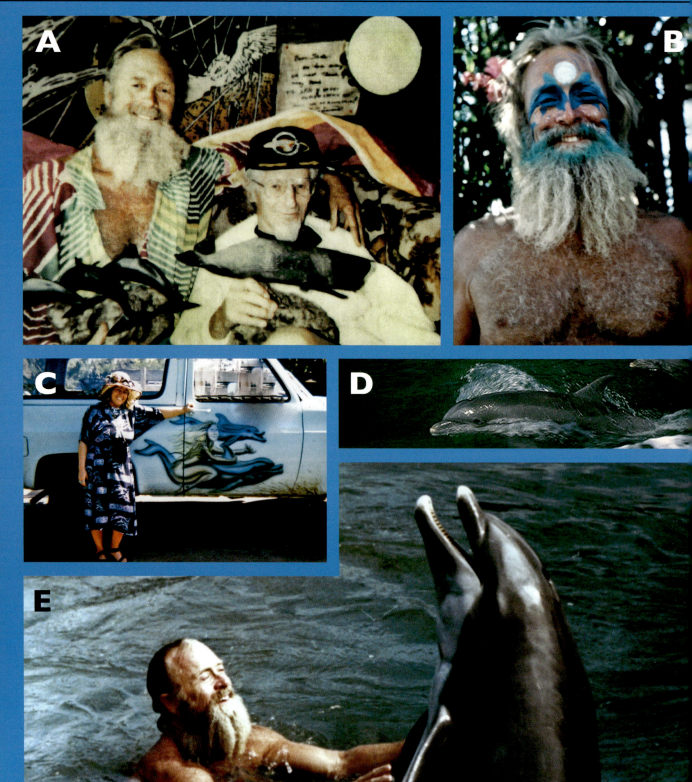

11 - extreme life life in the trees

12 - under water

13 - under water   life in the trees

14 - making her-story

life in the trees

15 - pirates, ships, and fish tales life in the trees

16 - stream life   life in the trees

About the Photos
(continued)

10 – Cetacean Love

A "With Dr. John Lilly loving the many cetacean sculptures by Jon Perry" ("Beluga Wails")

B "Seeing the world through 'Dolphin Eyes'"

C " 'Clown Chakra' Lucy-in-the-Sky with replacement for my 'stolen car' "

D "Bottle nose having fun planing" ("Dolphin Mind")

E "Reveling together in the Florida Keys – 'Did you hear the one about …?' "

11 – Extreme LIFE

A "Laird Hamilton surfing Jaws" (photo: Patrick McFeeley)
National Geographic cover, November 1998

B "The Blue Pearl"
A.k.a. The Blue Marble, NASA image of Earth from Space

C "Tree Yoga" - My form going into "PS, My Downfall"

12 & 13 – Under Water

12 A "The Three of Us" (photo: Daniel McCulloch)

Notice the serendipitous heart shape made by my *ungrasping* hand and the dolphin's fin.

B "Lana Miller and friends"

Lovely Lana was my dolphin diving, traveling partner to underwater realms and author of *Call of the Dolphins*.

C "A Trio" - Francesca with Bottlenose Dolphins, Bahamas

D   "A pod of humans"–Hawaii

E   "Coming up for air"– Like cetaceans, we need it to breathe.

F   *"Pas de Deux"*–Young Megan and friend

G   "At the Bottom"

Dean Bernal and "Jojo" in Turks & Caicos (Providentiales Island). Jojo was very people-friendly, having no pod. She may have been released or escaped from a research project and was wanting company.

13 H   "Spotted Dolphins, Bahamas"
Blowing bubble rings to impress his girl

I   "Spinner Dolphins at La Perouse Bay, Maui"

J   "Spinners in the Bahamas"

K   "Bottle Nose Dolphins in the Florida Keys"

14 – Making Her-story

A   "Lahaina shoreline from the sea"

There's the banyan tree in front of the library, the locale of "Pliny's Revenge", and The Pioneer Inn where Meg and I celebrated our win in "Uke China".

B   "Flubby Meets Subby" in "Uke China"

Megan is concealing pink and blue flubbies, ready to launch and about to make *her*story, as opposed to *his*tory.

C   "Proud Papa"–c.1992

D   "Diana and her 'was-band' "–c.2000

15 – Pirates, Ships, and Fish Tales

A   "*Mycia* and *Hula Girl*, Meyers Chuck, Alaska"–2004
"Wandering Eye …"

B   "The *Mycia* under sail," the Inland Passage (Photo A. Burtt)

C   " 'Hal' and I with Younis looking on"–Hal's still in the loop.

D   "Below on the *Mycia*"
At my laptop writing "Wandering Eye …"

E   "Shakeena at eight with a 'founder' "
She too caught a fish, maybe the last of an iceberg.

F   "Capt. Morgan listening to fish whispers" ("… say what?")

G   "Boat bones of our double-ender"
Before she got stuck in the mold ("Archer and Lockyer")

H   "The Boaty Treehouse" ("… Thoreau's Toolbox")

The *Ficus* banyan tree that cradles her I planted from a houseplant that failed my Bonsai course. The design emulates the aft cabin of a square-rigged sailing ship. When Zen let me move in I paid him $11 a month for rent. It was here I wrote most of these stories.

I   "Grandson Zen swinging in his dinghy–'Aarrr' "

J   "Pirate Zen at six"–2000

16 – Stream Life

A   "Reading from the Book of Fins"–August 1976

In our "front yard," Gannon & Megan listen attentively as water rushes over basalt cliffs into King's Pool after a storm.

B   "Little Meg rescuing tadpoles"–c.1972

C   "Warm rocks at Queen's Pool"–timeless

D   "Zantar emerging from King's Pool"–June 2009

E   "Megan on rope swing-sequence"–2009

The pool is rimmed with basalt cliffs where water falls when the stream is flowing. A spring under the cliff always provides fresh clean water.

All these images reveal our daily blessings of living on a stream, as depicted in "Stream Walk", "Whose Fangs", and "Life in the Trees".

Mahalo to all the photographers, known and unknown, for this chronicle of our lives! (Please see Credits.)

And special thanks goes to Mike Neal for his artistry with these pages of photos.

Coconut Ukulele

"The chief danger is that you may take too many precautions."
— Alfred Adler

Uke China!
GLOBAL WAR NARROWLY AVERTED BY LOCAL ECO-GIRL ARMED WITH PINK FLUBBY
READ ALL ABOUT IT!!!

A gray, sleek, and ominous submarine lay anchored in the roadstead off Lahaina when Meg and I awoke aboard our sailboat at the dock. It was summer, a special time for Megan and me to spend time together. Meg, age eleven, sized up the sub. She imitated it, as she does all animals. Her face and body changed. Some subtle shifts: waves ran down her long unmoving sides. Her conning tower shunned the morning sun. Meg emerged from the merge with a message: "It looks nuclear to me, and if it were coming to visit you ... it might not be good news."

That's all I needed to know. I fired up the small outboard engine. She tossed off the lines and hopped aboard, as our little boat backed out of the dock for a date with destiny. We both could feel the call.

A vessel built to kill two hundred cities at a time with MIRVs* has got a lot of nerve, and it must have got on Meg's.

* MIRV - Multiple Independently Targeted Re-Entry Vehicles

She could easily coalesce a caper before breakfast. How can a dad and daughter enjoy their hot chocolate and marshmallows if the world's teetering on the brink? No way.

Meg knew this. I agreed.

We passed the outer buoy, Lanai to the far right, and gradually aimed our bobbing craft toward the sub. Sailors now tumbled from the conning tower like angry bees swarming to protect their hive. In practiced coordination they moved, quiet and quick, to wave us far away from the vicinity of their lethal and indomitable home.

I hadn't noticed, so drawn was I to the ever-changing color of clouds on Lanai, that Meg had armed and positioned herself with two jiggling flubbies–water balloons–a pink and a blue, the most dangerous kind, behind her back.

The most advanced weapon of the most dangerous arrangement–the Nuclear Nation State–showed its big white teeth like a menaced whale as a wave broke along the bow. Riflemen now emerged from the tower and took aim as a loudspeaker blared a warning to us, "Change course NOW!!"

"NOW?" I throw the tiller hard to port. Well, I'll be ... a sub? My goodness! "What a lovely vessel!" I exclaim. "What does it do?" I shout. "What makes it go?"

A little girl with her hands behind her back and her

bumbling dad are centered in hairlines of sharpshooter scopes. The little sailboat swings away, narrowly averting a collision. The impenetrable sub and her perturbed crew relax ... too soon.

Meg's arm comes from behind her back and **swoosh**, the blue balloon arches through the air ... now a sphere, now an ellipsoid and definitely locked into a parabolic trajectory. Time slows. The weapon seems to stop and hover at the top of its path, then plunge downward toward its mark.

"Incoming flubbie," a crewman shouts, no doubt a veteran of sailboat wars where such weapons are launched at one another from surgical rubber stretched taut between masts on parallel sailing boats. (That he recognizes our weapon speaks well for the crew.)

The pound of jiggling water and gram of rubber, like I say, seems to hover in the morning sun ... then narrowly misses the laughing deck of the impregnable craft. **Splash!** The Pacific is a pint larger. The sub snickers. The Pacific patronizes. The crew laughs, their tensions released. Again, too soon.

Impregnable? Perhaps. Lethal? For sure!

Undaunted, Meg's left hand now clutches the pink balloon and: 3, 2, 1, 0, Launch! **Swoosh!** There it goes into ballistic orbit. This weapon clears the Pacific ... clears the deck ... and crewmen on the deck ... and is heading for the conning tower itself ... is heading for the ...? Horrified hunter eyes leap from easy relaxation to helpless observance as the violent pound of water impacts the *one* small vulnerable zone–the Command Book!

Bloosh!   An edge shot!   Total soako!

It goes into the rack holding the book near the top of the once proud, unassailable vessel, breaking its aggressive spirit.

The Captain leaps to save the day's unread command: **Nuke China!** (we later project, laughing), but the ink of the "N" in the message has merged with the freed water from the flying flubby ... merged and slid soundless down the armored steel of the once proud sub and quickly reachs the sea.

Gone. Gone the deadly command. Lost forever. Liberated, the sub joyfully awakens from a deep slumber, longing to play with whales.

The Captain is furious!!! Shaking the strategic water from the soaked pages. Shaking the book dry in a panic. Shaking and shaking and swearing. Shaking his finger at us. Now he thrusts the middle long one skyward, shaking and pumping.

"Oh my!" He's pointing now in quick hard moves. A

bell is ringing. Loudly. The seamen scurry into strange positions. I look back, wave, and suggest they "Have a nice day!"

But they have had a horrid day and are no doubt thinking bad thoughts, like *getting even*! It's still early, and I'm not sailing by for a second try.

"It's a good thing," I'm told later by a sailor from the sub, while I booze it at the bar. "Captain fired up the nuclear-powered water cannon! It'd cut you off at the waterline at a quarter mile."

Now *that* would have ruined our tiny white marshmallows floating in our mugs of hot chocolate as we toured and tootled and toasted our victory. As it was, we rolled and bobbed in the morning swell, bouncing in our little boat back to its berth, fresh from *saving the earth*, ready for hotcakes now with coconut syrup and double butter, a Sunday breakfast at the Pioneer Inn.

But wait a second here. Time for some imaginative reflection: The Captain reads the fading command, **"Uke China!"** Well, he hates to do this to China, knowing how foreign musical instruments have changed history, but a command is a command. Stand back here: give me some room! The old history books are thrown out. **Splash!** We're making *herstory* now.

The *orange* button, a transformer mechanism, watches

the approaching finger: *Nuke Warhead* to *Uke Playhead*. The button is pushed. Oh yes, It's pushed! **Roaroarararar Rwwwww!** Now another button flashes *red:* **Launch Ready**. The same finger leaps. **WWRWRWROOOARKA BLOOOSH WHOOSH!!!** Gone!

Twenty multiple-targeted Intercontinental Ballistic Missiles cradling twenty-two thousand well-tuned coconut shell ukuleles explode from the shocked waters of the placid Pacific, as the syrup hits our cakes. **Vooshhh!** And on Meg's first hot chocolate re-fill the missiles attain apogee three hundred miles above Midway Island. And on her second (and "triple up the butter please on the cakes") the MIRVs explode into many missiles destined to put the old song "Ain't She Sweet" back on the charts.

All guidance systems are running true, and two hundred schools are in the crosshairs when **Ka-Whambo** the missiles pop open like piñatas, launch their loads, and disintegrate into parachutes.

And on my last re-fill twenty-two thousand Chinese school children are picking rainbow-parachuted ukuleles from out of the air and playing harmonious frequencies of oneness. *Aloha 'oe** never sounded so good!

* *Aloha 'oe*: May you be loved. (Pukui)

"People who don't have embarrassing stories are untrustworthy. Or at the very least, they aren't telling the truth."

– Suzanne Guillette

Pliny's Revenge: Geometry 201

Notes on the nature, efficacy, and application of concentric, defensive odors in aquatic naked apes

- "Judge not, lest ye be judged." *The Bible*
- "One cannot ridicule the ancients with impunity." Aristotle: 384-322 B.C.
- "It is good luck to let fall three drops of urine upon your left foot in the morning." Pliny, the Elder: A.D. 23-79, Roman scholar, from his *Historic Naturalis.*
- "C'mon, Pliny, good luck compared to what? To firing the whole load down your Levis?" Zantar 1935-? Still writing *My Historic Naturalis.*

I remember some nearly instant karma of mine in Lahaina. Strolling beneath the wide banyan tree to a sunset observation spot in front of the library, I recognized an old bum I'd seen for years, now sitting on the park bench. Poor fellow seemed shell-shocked from some past war. I was carrying two ripe mangoes the color of the sunset sky, and so out of the goodness of my heart, or perhaps the pleasure and excellence I might derive from feeling so vastly superior to this derelict, I called over, "Would you like a mango?" He assented with a nod of the head. Hey, we're all brothers under the skin. So I sat down next to him, and we began peeling our mangoes without further words.

Words, it turned out, weren't necessary and would have been a dangerous and foolhardy act. Just breathing, I almost lost consciousness. Speaking, while subjecting my reeling taste buds to an already overwhelming olfactory experience, might have taken me straight through *un*-consciousness to outright death.

Using my finely tuned instinct as surfer–where you are overwhelmed beneath an avalanche of water before you can take a breath and must not panic in the pummeling and long period under water before air is once again available–I shut down all sensory input mechanisms and guided myself, eyes closed, back to my feet. Feet did their stuff. Ten breath-holding steps upwind, then I gingerly tested the air with my left nostril, shut down for fifty more feet and was back among the living, sucking sweet O_2 deep into my lungs.

Like astronauts being debriefed upon returning from an alien land, I queried my offended senses as to what it was they had experienced. *"Brace yourself,"* they warned. *"Pliny is to street people as street people are to yon sewer personage."* Whoa! My senses, which always speak in mathematics, tried again. *"Roy's boots are to Limburger cheese as Limburger cheese is to yon aromatic blight?"* My senses, inadequate to the task, threw in the towel. Quits!

Let my mind give it a try. Dear reader, say that you never took your pants off or down for any reason, their sitting area being totally intact (no rear flaps, unlike kid's jammies), and months passed. Get it? Whoa, think about it! Totally transcendent odor. Block clearing odor. How, in what frame of mind, had I been able to penetrate this lethal defense to deliver the mango? God knows: I don't.

But consider me, this lover of hoboes, severely chastened. Without hesitation, I thrust this slightly mobile rotten sewer of a man to the bottom of the category of Bum. Nothing personal about his Godhood, you understand: it might have been Jesus Christ testing me, but if so, that dude had lost one convert. He was flung forever from the glorious realms of hobo-hood and shouldn't for one minute even consider entrance through their hallowed portals.

Having delivered this damning judgment, some bell should have rung, when Om-ing cross-legged and bathed in the glorious light of sunset, an old whale prankster buddy, Greg, and his wife Krista, strolled up. Greg had toured the USA with FLO and me and returned to the islands to start what became a successful foundation to protect whales, edging into insignificance my tiny organization, the Cetacean Relations Society. They offered to buy me a drink.

"Okay, but the smallest bottle for the three of us," I said, and Krista hurried off to make the purchase.

Greg and I reveled in our past whale-saving capers, and oh, yes, today was the anniversary of my family's coming to Hawaii fifteen years earlier. Forget that my sister had died, my son had drowned, my marriage dissolved, and my only cherished daughter whom I adored was living with her mother on some faraway island. Hey, life goes on.

Krista reported back with a pint of rum, not the half pint that I had requested to be shared three ways. A pint …

"Oh, no thank you," they said, "we don't drink."

Well, who am I to be drinking when my friends aren't? I got this awkward stage over immediately by drinking the whole thing straight down, right then and there.

I awoke eight hours later at three AM in the black of night, alone, sprawled face down on the library lawn. I staggered to my feet to survey the ruins of my domain. In an area of thieves and rip-offs all my belongings were safe within a circle whose radius was equal to my height and seemed to be composed of rum and yesterday's lunch. Aha! Then that would account for the many different layers of finely wrought mud, grass, and vomit that encrusted my face, flaking off if I so much as blinked. My body, with its good surfer's sense, must have rolled over and away from each fresh deposit, lest it drown.

I further noticed a damp concentric circle, the radius of which was roughly the length of my leg, buzzing with flies, and composed also of yesterday's lunch, but which had chosen another exit in its eagerness to be done with me. This, I reasoned, must account for the bulging weight around the seat area of my Levi 501s! Alas, the vertical position that I had assumed by standing had some drawbacks, as aforementioned bulge heartlessly obeyed gravity and rushed to displace the air in my boots.

Whoosh! Whoosh!

Stunned, my nose submitted a report on a combination of odors vaguely reminiscent of someone I had met recently but was unable to recall. Further chastened, I slunk sloshing through the black starry night to a blessedly vacant waterfront where I united with a harbor hose, contributed my fair share to the polluted harbor waters, gave my clothes to the dumpster, and walked naked on the beach three blocks to my car. Hearing all the while some vague, reverberating laughter coming from what seemed to be the clouds, I finally regained my humor at the wisdom of Pliny's revenge.

"Life expectancy would grow by leaps and bounds if green vegetables smelled as good as bacon."

– Doug Larson

Indulgenous

"Listen up, Your Indulgency!" Indigenousity re-visited.

Cultural anthropologists have recently zeroed in on trans-cultural attributes that define humanity. Now, this *transcultural* is a rather large and important word. No more hanging up on some ethnic, racial, religious, or political difference. *Transcultural*: commonalities above cultural. Perhaps even transHUMANcultural.

One scratches one's head to imagine such a property. If just one person wouldn't do it, it's not transcultural. We think of the big Mambas and the small mambas, distinguished by wearing different length penis sheaths. Would the pope? Nope! At least not in public. Penis sheaths fail the transcultural test!

We think of Spanish bullfights and Creole Mardigras, Brazil's Carnival and solemn religious observances, but "No," my friend, the cultural anthropologist says, "transcultural is way beyond these specific observances."

"Okay, I give," I said, thinking what beyond eating, sleeping, reproducing, and eliminating remain?

"Singing?"

"No," his grave head shakes.

"Dancing?" I suggest.

"No."

"Drumming? Painting?"

"No, no."

I'm growing tired of the game. Now I *have* to know. "What?" I ask with a tone in my voice suggesting that it better be good … or else!

"It's an addiction." He says. "Moreover, a *willingness* to addict."

Flashback: a list of drugs swims through my mind, maybe still even in my head: I am grudgingly relinquishing my drugstream to that old do-gooder, *blood.* LSD, Ketamine, peyote, marijuana, ayajuasca, mescaline … None of these seem common to all cultures, yet all seem common to mine.

"MacDonald cheeseburgers," I suggest, having heard that they are enjoying a rather rapid cultural dissemination.

"Closer," he suggests.

"Burger King Whoppers?" I offer, salivatingly (flame broiled and all), hearing rainforests crashing to the ground.

"More basic," he hints.

"Salty fibers?"

"Bingo!" he says, "one half out of three."

Now I'm moving, but I've got to jettison half, either the *salt* or the *fibers*. "Fibers flunked?" I query.

"Flunked," he says. So he's saying there is a transcultural willingness to addict to salt.

"Mangoes," I slurp, remembering having heard Buddha died of such an overdose.

"Nahh," he explains, "mangoes aren't transcultural. They're …"

"Paradisiacal." I suggest, getting even. He nods. Two to go, I'm thinking.

"Sugar?" I smile sweetly.

"And fat," he adds, "*sugar, salt, and fat.*"

"Wait," I say, "where would Eskimos get sugar?"

"From the store," he says. "A willingness to addict, or an inability not to addict."

I must confess I had higher hopes than this for human transculturality, thinking perhaps of some universal search for religious fundamentals, peace of mind, peace of peoples, or at least what Bill got caught doing. But as I chewed over these mindless chomping transculturalities, some other major earthquake of an understanding lurched into my awareness.

It was a big game idea for sure: I could feel it. So I straightened my back, aligned my feet, breathed deeply, and invited it in. I scanned my mental horizon slowly and quietly, not wanting to frighten off the quarry. A hot pink color swam by. Letters on it. I threw the fly out far into memory lane, line looping, to a swirl by a shady branch next to a small waterfall in the rushing river. "Bright Pink" took it, and after a brief tussle I netted it and turned the letter side over.

Pink letters screamed "INDULGENCE" vertically exploding from a pile of pecans encircling a pecan-studded captured cookie on an elegant, vertical, gleaming black Safeway cookie bag. I remembered having stomached all the cookies, being labeled VERY BUTTER PECAN–in white, and with a whole line for VERY–and saying SELECT and PREMIUM QUALITY and SAFEWAY in gold, and I had found myself unable to discard the bag. I'd folded it and slipped it between two of my favorite books. The bag had made my most treasured possession category in less than one bite.

How had I happened on it? My best buddy, Eona, had thrust the swollen bag through the door of my lonely writing room one dark, rainy night and blown my mind with the contents and beauty of the bag. We had marveled at the taste and the Madison Avenue marketing genius, slyly decoding its seductive effectiveness: pure sexuality. But that's another story. Back to my thick-maned transculturalist scholar.

"Indulgence!" I offered explodingly. *That's* what's transcultural! Fat, salt, and sugar just create an opportunity for indulgence.

"Hmmmm," the great shaggy-haired cultural anthropologist uttered, meaningfully.

And then my mind made the leap across the great chasm … … INDULGENOUS PEOPLE!

Weren't we all transculturally indulgenous people, given the chance? That old "indigenous people" label had been creating havoc with the modern mind. Hadn't we all once been indigenous people, living off the land? Weren't people just people? Would you give indigenous people an "A+" for ecological behavior, for not having destroyed the earth? You could only do so much damage with a sealskin canoe and a sharp stick. Given the chance, some of those indigenous people are now going after whales with speedboats and machine guns. Were we *now* to bow to their wisdom for not having *then* radioactively contaminated the rolling blue sea?

Humans collectively indulge and overindulge whenever they can. This reverence for the unique wisdom and nobility of indigenous people took its place in my mind with all the other misunderstandings irrelevant to an accurate assessment of our world's critical condition.

Bake sales for battleships? Maybe. But Safeway just may have the successful marketing tool for world peace: overindulge in cookies and sex. Then war is a no-show.

At last, "indigenous" defined: the people who were waiting for indulgenous opportunities but hadn't had their chance. Yet. I hope they get it. Those cookies are terrific. In a sort of fatty, sugary way, they're worth their salt.

I checked the bag's serving size: two were suggested. Fat chance! There were twenty-two: that's eleven servings, the master number, 11. I had proven my mastery and necked down the whole bag–Kabblammo!! And Eona his. And we were glad.

It doesn't work to indulge and not be glad.

I checked the flattened gleaming bag's ingredients' claim for fiber and Vitamins A and C. Zero. If they had any redeeming qualities it wouldn't be indulgence. So until we can become *indulgenous*, we'll just have remain *indigenous*.

Heaven forbidgenous!

"You have to decide early on which is true: the Universe is either for us or against us."

– Albert Einstein

Homo bogus bogus

Megan had given me a free ticket to the Mainland. The only problem was that it was in her name. I would have to pose as Megan. But then that sounded impossible–her dress didn't fit, her spiked heels were too small, and the angle was all wrong for my lower back. Besides, I didn't have them with me. So I tried several Scottish brogue pronunciations of my new name, Megan: "Meegaahan … Maygane … Meeegone?"

There could be a totally natural gender naming confusion in some such brogue. I tried looking in the mirror and speaking an unconvincing accent in the airport john. I introduced myself as "Megan" in different ways, as I walked toward the ticket line.

It wasn't working.

I was in Honolulu without enough money to get back to Maui. Something would save me. It always does. I had long depended on not only the kindness of strangers but also the kindness of the workings of conscious Nature to help me.

But I had to really squint my eyes a little to see what would be the trajectory onto that plane. First, I looked at five long lines of people and sliding suitcases, inching forward. One ticket girl looked a little like Meg.

That's the line! Then an overall look at the lines reveals a very large and official looking TV camera and crew three lines away. They seem to be interviewing people. I wait and watch and then wave my ukulele in the air at some exact instant, and the TV crew drifts towards me.

I have now come within two people of the ticket clerk, and I've just decided to tell her the truth: it's my daughter's ticket; it had been bought because her grandmother was sick, but she had been sent an even quicker ticket, freeing this one, and this was my way to join her and her grandmother in her final hours. It must sound like a common lie, though true. Well, would truth see me through?

So now the cameras are on me, and of all things I'm being asked for my reaction to this being the last flight of World Airways! (At that moment I felt that if they'd asked me for a grandstand save of the airline last week, I could have worked that in, too.) So I sing my specialty *universal-for-any-situation* three-chord song, turning it into a rhyme, looking deep into the camera, into the eyes of the TV watchers themselves, and assure them with soothing tones in song to please remain seated, for this is not the end of the world, but merely the end of World Airways.

I end with a flurry of chords. Timing is perfect. I place the ticket–plunk–on the counter.

"I liked the song," the ticket angel says, looking puzzled at me and my ticket. "Thanks for the assurance that it is not the end of the world, only the end of World Airways, and the end of my job. And since it is, I'll accept your bogus ticket. You're the poetry man! Have a nice flight!"

"How could one not love such goodhearted disregard for convention?"

—Todd Swan

Dr. Tabbo

Dr. Tabbo lived and traveled with a small, white cockatiel living on top of his head, named "Kahili." "Dr. T" cared for people continually, excluding himself. I think the bird was there to keep the care and love flowing when no one was around to be massaged or perforated by his acupuncture quiver. They were never apart. "Dr. T" was extravagant with his love, and the bird received a lot of attention. Often, it was the wrong kind.

A cockatiel is no condor when it comes to cats. Kahili would quiver under the steady onslaught of a feline's gaze. But before we proceed to the *denouement* of the embattled and encircled bird, yes, I can feel your concern about Kahili's toilet habits while nestled and clinging to Tabbo's wild mane. Me too. Not Tabbo! "T" made a strange and convoluted case for dandruff control. He was the only person I ever met who preferred bird shit on his head. Most of us would opt for dandruff and pick up some bottle claiming "control" on the way home. In Kahili's realm, the dandruff might have met its match, but unfortunately so had Tabbo's social acceptance quotient.

But T was high, really high–stratospheric actually–every time I saw him. Agreement on his highness derived from explosive visits in his manic phase, combined with heroic and continual hits of acid, making his social presentation ... uhhh ... well ... perhaps an example would help.

T was "acid-stronomically" high, like I said, always. Except for this once, when he was low, *really* low. Face down on the floor. An unsightly floor, bare plywood stained with food and mud.

After a wild midnight visit of singing, philosophy, and obvious lies that had raged on toward sunrise, I sprang from my warm bed at the crack of noon to survey the damage. I found him face down on the floor of the outdoor kitchen. Face down, while my six cats circled his head and Kahili crouched behind a major tangle, visibly shaking. Whether thin feathers and the "unwholesome damps" of his locale, or the one hundred and twenty claws and six sets of jaws caused this shaking, we may never know. Flashing fangs numbering in the hundreds could have contributed to his anxiety, as well. Like I said, we can only speculate.

Kahili would have been history for sure, but Tabbo's

clever cat evasion measures must have been applied hours earlier, for an army of a million ants swarmed over nine cans of tuna and their fragments covering everything. Just the cans and their sharp lids everywhere made safe motion problematic for me. But *my* nine cans of tuna? My one defense against the end of the world, protein in a can, had been consumed. Resigned, I relaxed, sat down, and surveyed this unusual scene.

Number one: the bird looked worried. She had cause. Cats were thinking dark meat dessert after a heavenly orgy of more white meat tuna than they could have ever known. Indeed, this was Kahili's meat's darkest hour. Perhaps they should have dealt with their insanely rising expectations like a man. But they're cats. (We're worse.)

Number two: Tabbo was snoring loudly. This *might* have conveyed consciousness and aggression to the bright-eyed circling felines, as they studied Tabbo's unique presentation.

Number three: I couldn't help myself. I poured a half bottle of beer full of drowned flies and a struggling cockroach onto Tabbo's head for Kahili's sustenance or company, then started the coffee.

He leapt to one knee, groaning. Kahili cheered the

added height, and you could see the cats' spirits plummet. Weirdness had always been Tabbo's defense, as well as being strong as an ox and a wrestler. You wouldn't want to tangle with him. Unless you were his bird-shit-hair.

This lighthouse-and-scout-nature of mine looked for fallback positions for civilization, if momentum were lost. Business had won the world because it relies on man's competitive nature, as well as providing some short-term safe and repetitious movements for idle hands that so often inadvertently do the work of the devil. Long term safe? Red warning lights flash like Hotel Street, and a cacophony of warning buzzers sound like a whacked hornet's nest. If business stumbled, which it seems to be doing, idle hands will get back to the same old thing that kept the world's populations so low for so long–finding ways of killing each other. Civilization, never more than a thin veneer, was being forced to settle for a weather-beaten patina. And that was quickly eroding from the winds of change and acid rain.

Tabbo and his bird were a symbol not unlike the canary in the mine. Hours earlier, he was in the catbird seat as he eviscerated contemporary civilization. But here, a few hours later, a few small puffs in the winds of change all his own, he is face down. Far from being in any catbird seat, he's the toilet seat for a cat-scared bird. Toilet seat for a bird wildly pooping on a whole new zone, opposite the face. T's head is hanging, as cats circle closer.

It was a disturbing vision, yet I clung to it. Tabbo had attained his other knee, and only two cats flicked their tails, measuring for a leap to his head via a glance shot off his rising face.

I put his coffee on the floor.

"Yargghh ..." he yelled, struggling to one foot, cats scattering. Coffee was running down the wall, the cup ricocheting like a billiard ball. Wake up call, different from most. Surveying the mess, I blinked and smiled and reached for the fire hose. Tabbo ... one of a kind.

This–a snapshot of our times–is even worsening for many: face down in barf, cats circling your best bird, and ants laying up their winter stores at your expense. The cockatiel would have traded for a mineshaft, gladly.

A few like myself nail on shutters and braces as the barometer falls. The cockroach revived, leapt from Tabbo's locks, and made his escape. One frisky, radiation-proof survivor: that too was a disturbing omen.

Ready for anything!

"Admit that your own private Mount Everest exists. That is half the battle."

– Hugh MacCleod

PS, My Downfall

Two mini-marathons, an ironman training, an inter-island windsurfer race, four days straight of deep diving for hours with wild dolphins, a quick two-day row across the world's roughest channel eighty miles to my remote Molokai sea-cliff property, so I felt easily capable of withstanding a grueling power shopping (PS) expedition with my sweetheart, Sunshine.

We rose early on that fateful day. I watched the sun rise over the crater. Penetrating. No clouds.

I ate, did a brief three-hour workout: stretch, weights, Kung Fu and Taekwondo, showered, shaved, slipped into my workout shoes, and sauntered down the center of the small seaside street, arms swinging, hand in hand with my sweetheart, Sunshine.

"The Rainbow Attic"–a shopper's paradise–was but a few minutes' walk. I watched the easy stride of my sweetheart, matched it, and we effortlessly glided together toward our destination.

We had planned this raid for a long time. Some money had come in, and a fresh consignment of clothes was said to jam the shelves. Clothes, long sought or unimagined, could manifest at any moment on those hallowed hangers.

A week earlier I had bought a gold lamé coat for eight-dollars that Elvis would have loved. It hangs on the wall. I'll never wear it. Sunshine likes fabrics, and that gold coat was pure sunshine. Sold!

The Rainbow Attic is a consignment store. These were rich people's rejects. A diamond might tumble out of some old pocket. What must have been a DKNY thousand-dollar sequined silver bathing suit cost eight bucks, like nearly everything.

I found a bomber bud roach in a silk purse within a lipstick case under a pile of toothpicks. Made sense. Mouth things. But the smell gave it away. The purse was good luck, so I bought it. It's on the wall with the gold lamé coat. Better *it* than a stuffed, glass-eyed head of some luckless lion, but still with some of the excitement of the chase. Nailed on the wall with a pushpin, not on the savannah with a thirty-ought-six.

Purse died with a roach, not a roar. Purse rebirth. Place for the bucks. And grass. Hidden among complicit toothpicks. Who would guess? Fits right in on the wall at Sunshine's "Aloha Lani Tantric Goddess Temple," with thirty other glittering costumes on the violet walls. *Aloha Lani,* The Temple of Heavenly Love. That gold coat would look great on a lion–if you had one. But upwardly mobile yuppie lions bounding gold-coated up the down escalator–are the last thing we want. But the roach was great!

These past hunting/gathering successes at the Attic, as well as some knockout deals at the Salvy, had built in me the momentum of a winner, a sort of shared camaraderie with other champions: Duke Kahanamoku comes to mind. The competitors are bunched up–way behind. It gives that special meaning to the word "champ." Way ahead. Power shopping would be just the latest of a long series of my recent triumphs.

I felt our matched pace quicken as my sweetheart, Sunshine, and I blew by the Attic's sidewalk sale fifty-percent off rack. Losers.

We slipped through the door, and I headed deep into the women's slack section. Let the cowboys fight over Levis. Women's slacks, extra-large, size 14, silk. Miracles happen here.

And one did. Immediately! Blue velvet tights, some

private dancer's special thing, one of a kind! I felt the clarion call to liberate these tights. They would be my signature human-dolphin, photographer-choreographer's underwater tights. And shiny with silver threads or something. Sparkling blue! Dolphins would be green with envy.

I took them into the changing room curtained section. Plop. Sunshine dropped six other things over the stall for me to try. I was already behind by six try-ons, and I just got there. Seven! Sunshine is power shopping. I'm way behind. But when the going gets tuff ... you know the rest! And now it's time to show my stuff.

I'll just slip on these tights to assure the perfect fit: they're mine, made for me. My own choice! Not just Sunshine's. I'll open with a huge success. First domino of seven falling. My choice. Undisputed champ in gals' realms, too! Hah!

I step out of my dropped pants and thrust my leg into the glittering blue tights ..., but it stops almost immediately. Odd? I stumble and hop around on one foot trying to get the dancer's stirrup thing over my foot. Stuck! I crash into the flimsy wall. Muffled cry of alarm from the next stall as the wall buckles. This is sacred space, and they have honored the silence. Only the cash register's bell interrupts the reverence of serious shoppers.

I fall out the curtain door naked into a huge rack of laced panties. Victoria's Secret? Panties have no fear of flying! Half do! The whole unit teeters, but I grab it, as the other half launches.

I leap back into my stall and regard my glittering lower left leg far below. Then hop on one foot and pull. Plop again! Another stack of things from Sunshine joins the growing pile. I'm way behind.

A moment of panic! Sweat explodes from every pore. I breathe deeply. Calm my nerves. Sitting on the low bench will eliminate the tricky balance problem with these tights stuck to my left foot. I sit down. Breathe. Brace one arm on my knee and reach way out to my distant foot and try to get the damn stirrup foot thing over my foot and up my leg. But it won't move. These aren't floppy bellbottom pants. I pull harder. Won't move. Stuck.

So I reach out with both hands, thereby giving up my cantilevered back support, and give a mighty yank with both hands, quick and hard, to surprise this maniacal eel with a death grip on my foot. The tights don't budge, but some connection of muscles to somewhere in my lower back *does*.

Writhe to my feet in growing pain and deepening shock. Try to get my left foot with long blue eel attached to go down the leg of my pants. Eel won't go. I wrap my pants around my waist and stagger to a nearby low back rocking chair dragging the glittering blue eel, teeth clenched …

The chair's for sale! I'll pretend I'm considering a purchase and lean back. I pull my knees up like a fetus to grab and dislodge the fierce eel, but the chair and I tip all the way over backward on my head. Crunch: neck sounds.

I'm wedged upside down against the wall in the men's pants section. Total humiliation! The blue tights have a death grip on my foot. I squirm. The waist and size tag fall into my face. Plap. I focus on the tag! I have been sabotaged. They're not size14: they're size 6!

Me and my dolphin diving dreams are blinkered back to reality. Totally inappropriate. Wrong fabric, wrong size, not even that stretchy. A child's ballet costume! Someone put it back in the wrong section. *I've* done that before. Careless karma payback maybe!

But I'm trapped, inverted. So I whimper for help! Sunshine comes to my rescue with her helping hands. They tip me over sideways. Some sleek girls I'd seen are snickering, helping the owner get Victoria's sweet secrets re-racked.

The chair turns over sideways on me. Crunch … something else in my neck. Someone pulls it off, de-eels me, and I pull on my pants, excruciatingly.

I have ruined my back for two months. "Two months if you don't move; six if you do," said the doc last time. It has happened before. I shuffle hunched and groaning outside to a welcome milk box seat by the fifty-percent-off-rack-losers. The ones I blew by less than three minutes earlier. Feeling one-hundred percent off now, myself. And lost. Under three minutes? First round knockout. PS, my downfall.

Can't even get to the parking lot. A friend backs her car over the sidewalk curb to me, helps fold me in, drives us home. I am in excruciating pain. Couldn't have walked. What an immediate life-changer.

Power shopping? Girls only. They don't stoop so low as a mere, inadequate Ironman preparation. Moms are unbeatable. But I'll get the wooly mammoth when I'm up and around again.

"The mind is everything. What you think, you become."

– Buddha

E.T. Mates the Great White Hunter

It was a terrible sound. It was an unbelievably alien and hideous sound. It was a sound of power so terrifying and so totally obliterating that no interpretation, no resistance was possible. This terrible sound and its otherworldly nature had ripped me from deep sleep into a black room where eyes were useless. I was hopelessly aghast, as I quailed, helpless in its otherworldly thrall, it thrashing but a few feet away from my head. No gathering of powers to resist was possible. Every act my mind and body made to meet this unknown challenge threw me for a deeper loss, and my sprawled, supine form accepted its demise at the hands or tentacles or whatever lethal swinging appendages my attacker possessed.

Earlier that evening I had rejected vehemently all possibilities of extraterrestrial existence being here on Earth. So as I lay most vulnerable, recuperating from my power shopping fiasco, it seemed fitting that this should be my doubter's fate.

My life passed before my inward eyes. My mind skipped denial, anger, fear and acceptance, moving directly into resignation. My life had been good, loving, long, and its length, which would be curtailed at some point, was at *that* point.

The hugely unrecognizable but somehow hollow, metallic sound was whirring directly over my head. From every angle, first this, then that, north, south, east, west, my attacker from all sides belittled any possibility of my defense.

Sunshine, my dear fragile and petite lover whom I protected at my side in her sleep, was attempting communication. How awkward and useless, yet brave and heroic it now appeared. My scattered senses put fragments of speech into a meaningful juxtaposition.

"I got you a bell for your beard," she was saying.

This statement seemed as distant from reality as the horrible bashing, whirring sound so close to our common heads. Perhaps I had descended somehow into the blackened, crazed interior world of the insane. I whined a strained and helpless whine.

I heard Sunshine get out of bed and walk into the wall. Crash. She's keeping a brave front in the face of sure death, my heroine, my savior, but she's lost like me. My buddy, Rod, the other guard at the Tantric Temple of Goddesses, whimpered somewhere in the dark.

"No problem," she continued, "I'll get the lights on, and you with your great height can reach up and get that string untangled." My mind yearned to re-experience reality, but I could find neither mind *nor* reality. Sunshine sounded reassuring, but "strings ... bells ... beard ..."? Nothing made sense. The ominous swish of the extra-terrestrial's overwhelming weapon sounded closer as I sat up in bed. I was still enblackened, but slightly emboldened.

Sunshine switched on the light.

My light-shocked eyes beheld a white, alien helicopter-like outer space vehicle with disturbingly many silver extra-terrestrial heads attached to its killing blades that had colonized our ceiling and raced wildly, screeching its message of "Death Now", loudly.

Sunshine switched off the overhead ceiling fan, a four-bladed white one made by Hunter. Somehow this alien helicopter's horrific whirring sound must be a mating cry! As the spinning slowed, I heard Sunshine laughing through her words.

"Yesterday, after I took the bell off the balloon for your beard, I put the balloon in the closet. I guess somehow it flew out and got its string caught in the fan."

The lusty, erotic E.T. spun slowly to a halt on the ceiling, the blur of its many heads resolving slowly to but one head: an alien metallic helium balloon that carried the deadly message emblazoned in red letters, "Get Well Soon."

"One day I will find the right words, and they will be simple."

– Jack Kerouac

Sharkbite

So I had my life so crammed full of the great ideas from a thousand writers, poets, singers, teachers, philosophers, and friends that my big, thick book couldn't help but be a "best seller." Get me some bucks for a new set of right side wipers and a spare tire for Prince Valiant, my old but dependable Plymouth.

But before I turned *my book* in and got a bank account for the money and began handing it out to folks and groups that could make a difference, I thought I'd better read one book on writing to make sure I had the gist of the thing. Maybe books should be ideas *eight* layers deep, and I had only got to *seven.*

Rode my bike down to the library. Got me one of those writing books. I can remember the shock of it now, Hemingway saying something like, "A book is good in proportion to the number of great ideas it leaves out."

Leaves out??? Whoa! Total depression. Confusion. But finally turned to total elation. Life is funny that way.

Waves, or something.

So here was my last thought, the last big wave I rode in on: my book will be *really good*, having left out that fabulous overflowing banquet of so many great ideas. I hustled down the aisle to the H's, *The Old Man and the Sea,* and just like he said, there wasn't one idea in the whole thing! An old guy catches a swordfish, and the shark eats it before he gets it home. The fish too big for the boat or him to small for the hauling, I forget which, probably both.

If that happened now, the old guy would pull out an AK47 and blast that misguided shark that somehow had mistaken the old guy for a *victim.* Not *him*! Probably pump a few rounds into the Swordfish's head, too, so he wouldn't be getting any last minute bright ideas with that big sword of his.

Felt like Hemingway had been that big shark that took a huge bite out of *my* book. Spit out all the ideas. That one stopped me cold–me coming home with a skeleton after all that effort of learning. Ernest Hemingway? Earnestly Hemorrhaginglyway.

But he must know what he's talking about: sold a lotta books and musta got a lotta bucks, I thought. So instead of re-writing my whole huge book, I wrote a computer program that I called "Shark: Idea Checker".™ Shark™ sniffed every sentence and paragraph, and if it smelled any ideas in there, it just bit and spit. Full-on predatory ideavore, ole Shark, editing the meaty ideas out.

Idea Checker made Spell Checker seem like some finicky, starry-eyed do-gooder quibbling over an extra "h". Like some new age fruitarian or organic breatharian, maybe. Filtered!

Then I had a clever idea! I'd feed *The Old Man and the Sea* to Shark™ just to see if Ernest had his head on straight. See if an idea might have slipped by me. "Scan with OCR – Select all – Shark™ – Go." The story survived intact. Not one little scrap of an idea in the whole thing. Shark lookin' starved. Mean. Watch out …

Mood like that, I was kinda afraid to see what ole Shark would leave of *my* book, nothin' but a skeleton? But I hit "Select All" and said, "Go" to Shark anyway, and then I laughed and laughed. Shark might have been a way better editor than me, but now he was belly-up, bloated on the bottom. Biter must have outrun his spitter. Backup bloated. Glazed eyes. Couldn't pull off a twitch. But Shark had got *even* for me and the poor, ripped-off old rowboat guy, so we couldn't leave him just lying there on the bottom.

Sooooo, the rowboat guy goes out to save the drowning, dying shark. Good old guys a few generations back might do that sort of thing. Save the shark. He dives to the bottom and sizes up the situation: tough call. The old guy is hoping the rough skin of the shark will keep the rope from sliding off his head so he won't have to go around his fins. But no, rough as sharks' skins are–their skins are teeth, you know– the rope slides off the shark's head, and the old guy'll have to put his own head almost in the shark's mouth to get that loop in the rope over both side fins, but with one last push he makes it. And this is all one breath-hold dive down there ... And he's beginning to lose consciousness, seeing stars and all. Lucky that shark wasn't just faking it, like the wolf in Little Red Ridinghood. Finally, the old guy bursts through the surface to sunlight and air, with shark in tow, a hero to us all. Gandhi? St. Francis? Total approval!

Now, ghost of the dead swordfish has shown up to save the shark. No hard feelings among fishes. But then, a shark's not a fish! (Cartilage. No bones.) New rules. Shark takes a coupla bites out of the swordfish's ghost ... just laying up stores for hard times.

Well, back to the shark rescue. It's a huge struggle against time. Sharks die without water flowing through their gills. The old guy is rowing the boat hard, towing the shark, to get the water flowing through his gills fast enough. Remember, Shark is too full of ideas to swim.

A storm is bearing down, and the boat is tipping dangerously, but the old guy is outdoing himself in some magic way. Like that mom who lifted the truck off her pinned kid. But it's still not enough speed. Tragic ... eyes glazed ... near flat-line on an EKG readout ...

Storm hits. Lightning. Thunder. Mammoth waves. Whitecaps like Niagara. Yet in the midst of this unimaginable maelstrom, the old guy lashes together fish poles for a mast and ties up his clothes for sails – shirt off his back for the mainsail, pants for a double jib. The boat picks up speed, and then Shark comes all the way up and out and begins skittering across the face of this huge wave, smiling and wide-awake!

The shark and the old man and the boat do cranking bottom turns up and down the face of the wave, always keeping the rope taut. No slack. A miracle!

[Forty-five more pages, great rides, not one idea.] Storm passes. Music soars ... It looks like a whole new era of inter-species relationships is birthing: peaceable kingdom, shark and man, and a new day dawning ... But no ... screech,

screech, screech, scary music!

The old guy has finally bailed dry the sinking boat when WHOOSH, Shark barfs a ton of ideas into the old guy's boat, sinks it, and eats the old guy, but not his skeleton. Just like the Swordfish. Shark™ is picky, that way.

But the old guy's skeleton mysteriously sticks to the side of the shark. Tangled fishing line or something. Karma, maybe. Shark heads home to his family and explains the adventure.

"Right!" they all nod, smiling wickedly, having noticed the clinging skeleton, sizing up Shark™. (Sharks do eat bones, too, along with hubcaps and other underwater morsels, all except for Sharks™, programmed to eat only the meaty ideas.) Listening, an old Freudian shark whose frown reveals he senses an anal-retentive symbology somewhere in this recurring skeleton theme–retained perhaps in some linguistic realm–suggests to those gathered that sharks, too, are Time's quarry, caught in Its crosshairs of pearly teeth, and this skeleton we see could sooner or later be our own. But no, the unschooled schools of post-modern sharks aren't going for it, so the psychoanalyst shark quiets and later quietly bites a dreaming fish gliding by.

Come to think of it, I think Earnest's one-line advice–

the idea to leave out ideas if you want a book to sell–the idea that got all this going in the first place, *flunked its own test.* Shark bait, for sure. I turned Shark™ loose on Hemingway's big sentence about leaving out ideas, and all it left was "*A...*" hanging by a thread.

"When life gives you lemons, you make lemonade."

– Dale Carnegie

Glaucoma

My writing capacities soar after winning big at the writers' conference. Four days straight I write like I am a channel of information with abilities pouring in from every direction, even writing styles of different authors. It is reminiscent of my deepest cosmic experiences.

My mind says that I have become a nexus or tunable laser, a variably resonating chamber. Something in me can shift to catch the frequencies that name-brand authors caught.

My powers have gathered, and the big fish that I sought all through my youth is brought to the surface four times. Each time the computer goes blank at about midnight, and the next twenty-four hours are spent trying to recapture it. After four days of eighty hours of writing lost, I explode. I vent my disappointment to my friends. My eyes are red. An eye doctor is suggested.

I go for contacts. The doctor gives me a test for glaucoma and says, "Mr. Loomis, you're going blind: you've got

GLAUCOMA." He says glaucoma is excessive pressure from buildup of the fluids within the eye.

"No," I tell him, "it's only a temporary side effect of the wrong software on my computer. I'm writing a *magnum opus* on a Notepad™. The Notepad chokes and tosses in the towel at seventy kilobytes. Un-cried tears from loss of so much material."

"No one knows what causes it," he says.

I tell him again. Maybe he didn't hear me. Maybe *he* needs a hearing aid. "It's simple," I repeat, "Un-cried tears."

He charges me a hundred dollars for the advice and wants me to come back in two weeks. I do. The pressure is up. A hundred dollars more.

My daughter and ex-wife get a loan and buy a computer that won't choke and loan it to me to finish my book. The doctor insists on a third check-up. The pressure is gone. No glaucoma. False Alarm! Did I cry? No, I got a new computer. A hundred dollars more.

I've discovered the cause of glaucoma, and he's charged me three hundred dollars. I'm thinking of the Nobel Prize in Medicine, splitting the million with someone who maybe cured some world plague like AIDS, and he's thinking of the three bills.

You got glaucoma? You got three choices: 1) cry, 2) get a new computer, 3) pay off the doc's Mercedes. I did the last two. Do the first two: that's my advice.

The cause of my glaucoma was un-cried tears. My relief is a new computer. He wants three hundred dollars for giving me bad advice. Can I charge him for the trauma he caused me? Or my brilliant medical research? No, he charges me three times for his error. Go figure.

Anyway, I've survived the doctor bill (another loan against my future million). Don't get me wrong; I like the guy: he's a nice person.

And here's a strange-fluke: I've just met this beautiful, blind man named George, just when I'm getting diagnosed as going blind. He's writing a book, *The Joys of Blindness*. Okay, so the strange-fluke has gotta be worth the three hundred dollars! Right?

"For it is in giving that we receive."
– St. Francis of Assisi

My Stolen Car

I sit looking through the window to my lovely new chariot. Chariot of the gods? No ... the pods. Chariot of the pods! The dolphin pods.

My chariot is here. At last! It came embedded in a love letter that's sky blue with dolphins swimming on it with happy smiles and gleaming eyes ... like they just got laid or are planning on it.

The girl riding the closest dolphin on the door could well be my daughter. Her hand is giving the Hawaiian *shaka* sign. The thumb and little finger protrude and the three middle fingers fold inwards. Do it! Now wave your hand from side to side. "Shaka, brah," we in Hawaii say, smiling.

Back to this sky blue love letter, wrapped in dolphins and a totally fit, beautiful blond smiling mermaid daughter riding a dolphin and giving us the *shaka* sign. Today on her birthday she announced that she had finally found after twenty years something she'd been wanting to gift herself. Some aspect of self-love had apparently matured. These are things a father likes to hear.

"What is it?" a rather large band of playful birthday celebrants asked.

"Outside," she said.

We followed her with growing expectation to the door. What *was* it outside? A big plant? The entire outdoors? Space? Endless time wrapped in Snickers wrappers? God herself in a limousine going shopping for roses?

Light flooding in the doorway carried an unsettling reality: my car had been stolen. My reliable Plymouth, "Prince Valiant," GONE! All my life–all my years of writing, computer, wallet, credit cards, fins, mask, snorkels–gone, in my stolen car!

Some other vehicle was occupying its spot. Not a bad truck at that: an immaculate twenty-year-old, diesel, war–surplus truck, freshly sprayed baby blue, and with a pair of exquisite dolphins painted on its side by my friend Dolphin Dave. I'd know his artwork anywhere. Well, I'll be if Dave hadn't just painted over the empire's skulking-toxic-camo-colors with his buoyant dynamic dolphins and my dolphin–diving, riding daughter!

So there it is, and with all my "stolen" stuff inside. Radiating love in the fresh rain. Radiating a daughter wanting her father to have a dependable, unstoppable four-wheel-drive, kick-ass truck for his wild and rugged waterfall lands, and with his own happy mermaid daughter on the side riding a dolphin and waving *shaka* to the world.

    For twenty years! Some love letters take a long time to deliver.

The fabled "Mahina"

"I like nonsense: it wakes up the brain cells.
Fantasy is a necessary ingredient in living ...
that enables you to laugh at life's realities."

—Theodore Geisel

Whose Fangs?

There had been a Blessing Way a week before Megan's first birthing. It was at Danya's Medicine Wheel, a short walk away, where there was a big, cozy teepee–her home–and a great sweat lodge. (Hippies playing Indians or haoles in love with Nature, either way–just great.) And all this overlooking the ocean and our favorite pools, rope swings and waterfalls: our *daily* blessings.

We had dug a huge hole to cook the many yams, sweet potatoes, cassava, and turkey for Thanksgiving. The food was all wrapped in banana and ti leaves and buried underground with many red-hot rocks for cooking that had been prepared in our campfire.

A dozen children are sitting and sleeping around the dying fire when I get there at two in the morning. I tune up my coconut uke and look for trouble. Expectant little ones awaken and glow, their faces gleaming in the moonlight. The old bearded Santa is here: Santa has come.

We all look at each other and smile a long time. I am collecting from each all they need to laugh a lot.

"Where's the dog?" I ask casually. I hope there's a dog missing in someone's mind.

Children's faces turn like something might be a missing dog. I collect their delight and present it with a new question: "Where's the *turkey*?"

The children's minds are churning for the funnest connection and someone on the left thinks it … and it's out … and now their faces are *really* gleaming. I lift my coconut uke and croon:

"Whose fangs are those?

Sunk firmly in our turkey bird,

Speeding through the wetting weeds,

Heading for a showdown

With his naked ape

Who calls himself his master?

If he wants to taste that bird

He'll have to run much faster!

WHOSEFANGS? ...

Talkin' 'bout MY DOG ... MY DOG!

Talkin' 'bout WHOSEFANGS! ...

WHOSEFANGS!!"

"Whose-fangs" becomes increasingly funny because saying "whose-fangs" in the rhythm of the song blows a stream of air up your nose and tickles the hairs. And as "whose-fangs" edges into the round format of never-ending repetition, continuing laughter is assured.

    The children's wish for laughter
            has been granted,
  As we sing laughing into the night
            in ten changing laughish parts.

And our minds imagine the chase with
    his master losing ground,
And the looking-backward look
    in the dog's eyes …
And the soaking weeds.

And little eyes roll up in gleaming faces,
    all lips-agiggle,
Thinking of that poor bloke's chaps soaked,
    ever welshing through the weeds,
Turkeybird long gone from table,
    flopping from flapping jowls.

And then the real non-missing dog who is innocent, but having had his character impugned, howls at the moon as the turkey cooks deep in the Earth. And feeling blessed, the Humans howl at the Moon with the Dog.

"It is preoccupation with possession, more than anything else, that prevents men from living freely and nobly."

– Bertrand Russell

Owning Things

Paul had announced his arrival at my niece Shelley's quiet upscale Kaneohe waterfront condominium at one in the morning by a series of bloodcurdling hoots and howls learned from monkeys in some village square in southern India. The neighbors were impressed, the guards were called, and a dozen alarmed and sleepy faces noticed Paul slipping into our condo. New windows began lighting up rapidly, and then began to darken, as normality slowly returned–the location of the new personage noted and recorded.

Paul, way over six feet and seventy years old, was a phenomenon of physical and mental health, having done hours of yoga and meditation daily for decades. Years earlier, Gold's Gym had been his choice for bodybuilding. Now he traveled the world with an eighty-pound backpack and tent, wrapping his sandwiches for the day in freshly published newspapers of the area, being the cleanest wrap around. All this, and his relative, towering height, allowed him to walk into any remote village in any unpronounceable country, knowing no one, and make every day a success that was "totally different."

His early training had been telephone work in a Wall Street boiler room in which non-existent stocks were exchanged for verbally beleaguered customers' existent money. Dissatisfied customers of fifty years ago must have been rare in the remote places, such as he chose. Paul's salesmanship remained awesome but now was dedicated to ensuring survival. Our paths crossed in Hawaii, he on the way to Africa via the Solomon Islands, where he was going to attempt to keep his head among a tribe of headhunters up some vine-entangled river where no white man had ever gone.

Paul's obsession of the last forty years had been gurus, wherever they were. A convert from Catholicism–via Maharishi, via Rajneesh, and finally via a black dancer dancing on a black pedestal on a darkened theater stage wearing a black T-shirt reading in big white block letters, "FUCK WHAT YOU HEARD"–to wandering the globe *free*, pretty much like God himself, he had absorbed and enjoyed all human religious fantasies.

High in frame and aim–a laughing twinkly-eyed Buddha, or Zorba, or the next Savior himself–Paul walked together with me along the incredibly swanky, towering glass-walled buildings of Honolulu. Then at one point he experienced an epiphany that had him swirling and hysterically laughing with his eyes wide, looking upward at these gleaming glass giants. The crowds parted around him like water around rocks in a river.

I watched him in total enjoyment and finally found that I, myself, was launched into a hyper state, from which I then realized that–in that moment–Paul was God ... was God himself enjoying totally *His creation.* EPIPHANY PLUS!

I had fragmentary glimpses of the mechanisms that had created these improbably high accomplishments–all this from nearly nothing by an aquatic ape who had spent a million years stoked to find a clam, to these glistening towers of opulence. I found my mouth uttering what seemed an impossible question, "How did *You* do this?"

Yet, it was the correct question, and one that took no reflection whatsoever on Paul's part, although the delivery of the answer was of course unique. He spun and launched one laughing word per revolution: "Jimmie ... Jimmie ... it ... was ... so ... easy ... I ... just ... let ... them ... ha ... Ha ... HA ... HA! ... **OWN THINGS!**"

Cat-Man-Bliss

"Catmando" - A Soft Shoe Shuffle

(80 bpm – feel in 2)

[spoken to guitar vamp]

We've had six kittens at our house lately –

Catatonic, Cataleptic, Catastrophic,

Catapult, Catamaran, and Catmando [Katmandu].

This song is about Catmando, and the

Needs of yours that he can fulfill.

Intro:

[sung]

I've got a little friend that you might like to meet,

He's orange as a carrot, but a hundred times as sweet,

And if you've got

Needs like these

Well, he's got solutions, and he loves to please …

    1.   Like if you're needing

              the magazine you're reading sat on …

                       Mando can do:

Or if you've needed
> the letter you're writing shredded ...
>> Mando can do:

He's the kind of cat who wants to know
Anyone else who's really goin' slow ...

So if you've been needing
> your trash sack whacked,
Or if you've been needing
> your Big Mac attacked,

Well, he's the kind of slidy sneaker ...
> he's gonna slip on through,
>> Mando.

2.   Like if you've been needing
> some silence instead of cheeping ...
>> Mando can do:

Or if you've been needing
> your shoulders leapt on and bleeding ...
>> Mando can do:

Got to turn the toilet paper roll
> to the wall,
Or Mando will spin it and simply
> unroll it all:

He's that kind of furry fella,
> Everything's more funny with ...
>> Catmando.

3.   [Whistle 4 bars]

Mando can do:

[Whistle 4 bars]

Mando can do:

And if you need
> some cat-size shade made,
Or if you've been needing
> your lady cat laid,

The cat's so apt; he digs the grooves,
> Mando ...

[spoken]

I mean he really digs the grooves.

4. Lies on his back and bats the tail of a stamping horse,
Sprawls in every doorway, and never moves, of course;

Been thinking of running for "Cat of the Year,"
If you're looking to find his tail
    you might check in your beer …

So, if you've been needing a dead rat
    in the bottom of your bed,
Or a half a dozen fleas crawling
    'round on your head,

He's our favorite furrying, purrying,
never worrying Catmando woo woo woo woo ooh!

[Spoken softly]
Hey Mando … my petting hand's itching for you!

(Music available at www.savingthecosmostiltuesday.com)

"No good deed goes unpunished."

– Oscar Wilde

Pet Scan* Ten? Nein, Eleven

As Bong Quixote at sixty-six retires to the Boaty Tree** alone for Summer A.D. 2002 to finish his book and achieve endarkenment, making sure that he has no commitments to limit his freedom, he scans the number of animals for whom he finds himself responsible. Only ten people have left him with their pets, so it should be a short pet scan.

1) Meg: six black ducks; one lame white duck; one cat, "Makani"; one Cockatiel, "Kahili", (a gift from Dr. Tabbo); one fish (Siamese fighting), "Bad Ass"

2) Dustin: one dog, "Mahina"

3) Diane: one cat, "Kamehameha", a.k.a. "Kamesters"

4) Kaimana: one cat, "Mufasa" (The Lion King)

5) Rico: one black cat, "Marcus Garvey"

6) Stephanie: one cat, "Ebony". She had a pit-bull, but it early disqualified itself by biting my balls on the opening intro. Gone! Balls? No! Dog!

---

* PET Scan – In medicine, Positron Emission Tomography (PET) Scan
** Boaty Tree – housing a boat in its branches where Quixote seeks endarkenment, as Buddha under the Bodhi Tree experienced enlightenment

7) Edmund Ling: only one blind, deaf horse, "Jiggs"

8) Shakeena: one cat, "Little Guy"

9) Sheila: one cat, "Precious"

10) Durien: one dog, Rottweiler, "Lani". (Shows her teeth and snaps them. That *is* a smile, isn't it?)

Can't take much time to deal with these critters, so let's take a look at how it's done.

At three AM from a deep and peaceful sleep I am awakened by two cats running full speed and deep clawed, accelerating across my face with a blood curdling, ear splitting escape yowl. That would be Mufasa, doing his bully Lion King thing. In the lead would be the cat who lives with me, Precious. Her nose got slashed: my face has nine bleeding claw prints.

I find flashlight and throw at Mufasa, thereby losing light somewhere in weeds. Reflect on how I can alter the Boaty Treehouse to keep all cats but Precious out. Think two hours about it; find a solution at the beginning of the third hour, but fall asleep and forget what it was.

Daylight awakens me, so I pee, wash out pee jar and replace, wash face and tame hair with some water, have a papaya and peanut butter, make coffee, and go to feed Diane's cat. In her abandoned house the carpenter bees are buzzing loudly and boring into roof rafters, threatening a huge roof collapse, so I swat two into Eternity with the badminton racket. Pow! Whap! Don't like killing them, but it's Diane's house, goddammit. Kamesters, whose territory it officially is, allows four other cats–Marcus, Mufasa, Little Guy and Ebony–to crowd him out of his bowl. So I take food up to my cat. She gets ripped off and chased out after a few bites by the same four slackers from Auntie Di's establishment who have buffed the bowl and bouffed.*** Another illegal B&B&B!

Next, I take on the black ducks, serve two scoops, then empty their pond and refill: fifteen minutes. White duck gets a scoop, and I get some nice feather feels: a nice resilient feeling and hollow sounding "Bop Bop Bop" on the lame duck's big breast. Duck hisses continually. I've gotten a little satisfaction and move on, bop hand tingling.

Give a scoop of cat food for Little Guy in outside table bowl. Mynabirds and doves fly in and ravage all that's there. Gone in thirty seconds. Bad Ass, the fish, gets a sprinkle of food and the haunch of a woolly mammoth from our freezer. (Or was it Costco cat food like all the rest?)

Quixote is leaving a string of happy campers in his wake, so he heads on down to the yurt. Makani gets a rub,

---

*** Bouffed – French for *puffed out, full.*

pet and kiss, water and a blast of cat food from a coffee can. Girl bird "Kahili" gets a water jar refill and some seeds added to her cage, as well as a little trip on my shoulders and head while I check for faxes of things Megan needs me to do for her. No faxes, but I read *Contrary Mary* and a Berenstein Bear book from the grandkid's bookshelf. Bears eat a lot: better to just read about them!

Downstairs to Dusty's dog, Mahina. Mahina gets dry food, wet food, and fresh bowl of water. She ignores food, so I unleash her. She needs exercise, so I put short leash on, and we run together all the way to the bridge, *her* pulling *me*. The Rottweiler, Lani, joins the crowd, adding menace, as I now get dragged, feet braced against the road, my running velocity exceeded. Upstream, we go from the bridge to waterfall pool, and a good swim and dog paddle is had by all.

When we return Mahina needs to be able to play with Lani, so they romp in yard for half an hour, and then I tie up Mahina. Her bowls are empty. She hasn't eaten, but Lani has. I pour more. Lani nails that, too. Free dog Lani nails all ground-level food–cat bowls, too.

Now I'm free to water my three gardens, and check on blind pony, Jiggs. Oops, he's in the garden: well, maybe the carrot tops will improve his eyesight. I lead him away, and he leads *me* to the banana trees with ripe stalks–good smeller. As he stands and munches the fallen fruit, I return to water the gardens.

Two hours have passed, so I take an hour nap. Upon waking, I work on shower house for Meg, and then do the animal feeding run and garden watering for the second time.

And that's about it for a day, with a few more naps and some writing, several hours of reading, two or three perhaps; and a little Internet to look up reviews and critiques of science books I've read about. And I've had a couple of one hour visits from friends. Check phone messages. Only two. Both from friend Daniel saying come up and get the dog, "Kiva," that Max has left for him–and now me–to take care of for three months. Pet scan ten? Nein, eleven!!

Question: What's three months?

Answer: Well ... the summer I had planned to be free.

Wait ... doesn't that make twelve disciples while I feed their multitudes? Serves me right for being a JC (my initials) here on Maui for thirty-three years. Thirty-three was a hard year for the number-one JC. Me too, when it comes to uninvited guests: three dogs, eight birds, six cats, ten wild birds, one horse, one fish, and two hundred bees. No wonder there was a last supper! Food ran out. And patience. (Food stamps, too, perhaps?)

**Read All about it! Pontius Pilate,
high judge and restaurant owner, busts local guru, JC,
for a twelve kids food stamp scam.**

(Gethsemane Gazette)

If the cock crows thrice and the Costco cat food be trayed, I'll be in the cave waiting for the stone to be rolled away while getting way stoned.

Warning!   Go Back!   Deep eschatological questions ahead.

Should I seek help figuring out what the problem is? My boundaries too permeable? Cells membranes are semi-permeable, but are mine totally? How have I let this happen to me? Easy! By being the stay-at-home gramps.

I do love the pet interactions for sure. They are great pleasures to be with, their sounds and smells and gaits, thrilling wild animals gone tame, like us. Bringing them food is fun.

I can imagine passing out this letter to all involved and just ask how they might help me reduce the squandering of my energies in Pet Hierarchy Battles. Nervous system shattering yowls explode daily at any moment over some Beta challenging an Alpha. Stuff crashes. Cherished statues break. Bad, mad mood rises.

That the damned animals wouldn't just all be delighted to be fed for free, but have to stage pecking order trips when I'm trying to enjoy turning them on to food and not fights?! Expectations of quiet gratitude unfulfilled.

These are God's problems. Why should I care?

Peaceable Kingdom Plan gone Belly Up, Binky?

Yeah! Damned pet power politics in Paradise! Who's number-one and who ain't is too much like the Real World.

Either pawn of paws-and-fur and beaks-and-claws
Or pawn of politicians?
A Pet of Power, or a Prisoner of Pets?
Pawn of both! Town or Country.
No escape.

Teetering on the brink of the next trillion
Years of You-less-ness,
Who would not enjoy feeding and being fed?
Bouffe unto others, as you would have them
Bouffe unto you!

Hark! I think I hear some unfed feathers flapping,
Some unfed fins a-swish.

Yours truly: one naked ape, "Jim," a.k.a. "JC,"
a.k.a. "Zantar," a.k.a. "Bong Quixote."

"Almost every wise saying has an opposite one, no less wise, to balance it."

– George Santayana

Too Much Love, Too Little Violence?

Dusty was gone jazz trumpet gigging to Kauai for three days, and his dog, "Mahina", missed him and performed uncharacteristic but ancient uncivilized behaviors, accompanied by "Marley", the neighbor's dog. Like catching a chicken and growling at people walking by so that they were afraid to go by the ferocious beast guarding her catch. Like even growling at Jeff, Mahina's friend, when he tried to pet her.

 I had been rousted while reading in the Boaty Tree by a frightened passerby, "Hello …? Are these your dogs?"

 "No!" I yelled, climbed down, gave Mahina a threatening look, took the big warm bloody, guarded chicken from the road, and threw it into the tall grass off to the side. The woman passed safely.

 "Too much love," Dusty says, in explaining Mahina's behavior.

 "And … too little violence," says me, a contrarian.

 Captain Cook, upon being charged by a Hawaiian

warrior wielding the very dagger Cook had earlier given him, shot the man with the one barrel of his gun loaded with *buckshot*–a warning shot–which didn't penetrate the warrior's protective vest. If Cook had used the *other* barrel containing a *ball*, it would have killed the warrior. Had they seen their lead man down for good, the Hawaiians *might* have stopped the momentum of violence that was building and reconsidered. In which case only *one* would have been killed rather than *twenty* in the ensuing melee, and–consider this–the Hawaiians might not have lost their land!

How's that?

Cook had taken pride in not hurting anyone, in using the least amount of violence to accomplish his task. His *lifeboat* had been stolen, and he was ten thousand miles from home with two hundred men depending on that lifeboat for their lives! Cook had gone ashore and was entreating the local chief to come out to his ship for a meal. The chief would of course be held until the lifeboat was returned. Said chief was used to coming aboard Cook's ship for dinner, but this was before breakfast. Off to a strange start.

This bartering-back-the-chief for stolen items had peaceable outcomes throughout the Pacific, but that day was an exception. The exceptional outcome was that Cook lost *his* life and the Hawaiians lost *their* land. The British abandoned their protectorate years later, as they reconsidered the situation of the Hawaiians having killed their famous navigator.

An historical note: the British did not typically take the land from the inhabitants of their colonies–India, for example–but Americans did. This raises an interesting question: if there can be too much love, can there be too little violence?

That the Hawaiians lost their land because of too little violence on Cook's part is an unusual take, yet it reveals the subtle complexity of anything involving humans. The right amount of love so as not to turn violent in its absence, and the right amount of violence–or threat to prevent violence–so as not to lose love, is the continually changing balance that humans seek ... and often miss.

Since I equate Love with Civilization (memorized love), I ask, "How thick is the veneer of Mahina's civilization?"

Four days, I'd guess. Three, with Marley. A day less per additional dog.

With humans? Microseconds, I fear. Touchy ape. Unpredictable, too.

I asked Dustin to summarize the growing quandary. What was needed?

"Fine balance," he said.

"Are these the exceptions that prove the rule, the extremes that legitimize the middle?" I asked.

"Check with Goldilocks."

Goldilocks wasn't around, so I got down on my knees and checked with Mahina, the fastest girl dog at Baldwin Beach Park–the one whose penchant for mob behavior with Marley, and whose eye-leg-jaw-tooth coordination had overwhelmed the formidable opposition of talons, beak, and evasive flight, devolving into a trail of feathers and blood, the one who growled at a hopeful pass-her-by whose frightened calls had interrupted my reading.

Mahina looked me square in the eyes. Her balance shifted.

I thanked her for turning off the four AM feathered alarm clock!

She sat down. And licked my nose.

As Goldilocks would say, "Just right!"

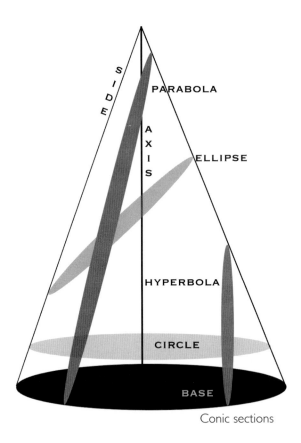

Conic sections

"Man's most human characteristic is not his ability to learn, which he shares with many other species, but his ability to teach and store what others have developed and taught him."

– Margaret Mead

More Than I Needed to Know I Learned in the Sandbox

Nothing was more fun in the sandbox than pouring out a bucket of sand slowly to form a cone, and then watching it have an avalanche. I could get it to a point where a little sugar sprinkled on it would bring ants, and the ants would create a landslide. It made a pleasing shape like an ice cream cone upside down, and the more sand you poured, the bigger it got. And kids like big cones ('specially chocolate).

Funny thing about it, big or small, they all had the same shape and organized themselves to that shape before the avalanche began. They hovered in this very special way, large or small, just before it slid down. A pile of coarser sand, or even rice or peas or beans would do the same thing, so whatever was going on, it wasn't about the sand.

But Mom's three-minute egg timer with the sand pouring through the little hole to the bottom and Dad timing it with his watch and having me write the times down and look at the slight variation in the times at dinner after dessert, might have made the whole *study* a kind of dessert for me. And sand came in two flavors—old shells and old rocks. I'd still take a sand pile that was a double helping of old shells, given the choice.

The sand cones were quick to get a couple inches high, but it took a long time to get an additional inch of height once the thing started getting big. But each time, as it got bigger, it would reach a point where it sort of hovered at being balanced, and then the slightest change could start an avalanche.

Sometimes just sitting there, doing nothing, it would avalanche on the inside and cave in a little all over. You could see it settle. Lots of little ones and a few big ones, it seemed. An outside avalanche, and the cone would start over again with a little bigger base (you know, where you put the ice cream in).

My dad, Joe, pointed out how the upside-down cone would be right-side-up for the folks at the antipodes. Those were the guys living directly opposite you on the earth if you bored right straight down.

Mom said avalanches happened in snow, too. Skiers had to watch out. There, *they* were the additional grain of sand on the pile that got the snow sliding, and they usually got buried and died.

I liked to hear my French friend say "avalanche". You heard the "launch" which I liked–ships and rockets and all–and you heard the word lunch, too, which I also liked a lot.

Something else: saying, "avalanche", sounded a lot like *an avalanche*. You say "A"–hardly anything–then "VA"–oops, getting bigger–the "A" rolled over to the other side–and "LANCHE". The way your tongue came off the roof of your mouth to go from "L" to get the third "A" sounded like things sliding, and the way your mouth finished up with the "CH", ... it was all over. Also, like a wave breaking: "A" the whitecap, "VA" the curl, and "LAUNCH", the impact zone. You didn't want to get "launched" into there–or you got lunched.

Dad said avalanches happened underwater, too, from earthquakes. Again, just a little change could do it, and folks living on the seacoast could find themselves for a few last moments looking at an avalanche of water coming their way fast. He said the same thing probably even happened on stars, too: "Star-quakes", he called them.

Then, he drew a picture of the sand cone on the flat sand and drew four different ways of slicing through the cone with their different curving shapes: a *circle*, a *parabola*, an *ellipse*, and a *hyperbola*. The *circle* made the wheel that made our growing civilization possible; the *parabola* described the curves of all things thrown on Earth–baseballs, bullets, and cannon shells; the *ellipse* told how Earth and all the planets moved around the sun; and the *hyperbola* described the comets' paths. The universe's main laws and shaped in a cone of sand … Wow!

So, together we were discovering some basic rules of Nature, first from the sandbox and then from the mailbox. Each month, beginning in 1939, we'd look forward to the *Scientific American* showing up, and each month we'd read that distinguished journal together. Waves and sand and snow and water and earthquakes and "star-quakes" were all somehow following the same rules–"the nature of Nature," Dad called it.

I vowed to find out what those rules are. That big effects could come from small causes was the weird part. Most stuff took a lot of effort to get big things going, but not all. Why was that? What was the difference? I promised Dad I'd keep asking these questions.

Years later, when I became Dad in the sandbox, I found myself asking those questions with *my* kids, and later with my grandkids. When my son, Gannon, asked what the song meant by saying "we are stardust, we are golden," we picked up *our* copy of *Scientific American* and read about those big exploding stars called "supernovas". Only they could make all the stuff we are made of. (Hadn't Dad said I was made from stars?)

"Well," Gannon said, "since 'super' means 'big' and 'nova' means 'new', we must all be *big light news*." He was our golden boy.

I learned more about what Dad had been getting at, something that came to be called that "exquisite balance place"–where the thing becomes one whole and has its own rules from within, where "everything is connected to everything else"–the place where life evolves. Not too hot, not too cold, just right, for Life. Dad was good with sand *castles*, too, but he aimed me at some mystery of nature that was being revealed in sand *piles*, that had to do with us *thinking about* sand piles.

"Some kind of strange *reflection* going on," he said, 'cause he could feel that *ideas* were avalanches, too. Find that mirror, that *mirror-cle,* was my goal. For Dad.

Here's a list of stuff I learned in the sandbox with Dad and then *as* Dad and Gramps:

1) Different things follow the same rules, so Nature has a *knowable* nature.

2) *Size* doesn't always count, but *shape* usually does.

3) Some things organize themselves into critical situations, where a little cause, *the tipping point,* can set off large effects.

4) Our elements come from stars, and they organize themselves into life on Earth.

5) We are that LIFE, looking for clues to what to do next.

6) Nature's nature organizes us to know Nature's nature.

7) Something self-reflective is going on in our galactic neighborhood, *Homo sapiens sapiens–us* thinking *about* thinking.

8) It is great to take on the task to find "what's up" and keep that goal *first.*

9) Don't skip Sandbox in kindergarten, unless you've got a good "sand-dad".

For "sand-dad wanna be's", you'll find the science of all this in Per Bak's book, *How Nature Works: The Science of Self-Organized Criticality.*

"Imagination is the highest kite one can fly."

– Jeffrey Sachs

Wandering Eye Takes "Hal" Out of the Loop

Prologue:

Now in Alaska with all the family, Jim finds his search for the conclusion of his halibut career beckoning aboard the schooner of his early childhood dreams. It's one big reason he has come: to wrap up the halibut cycle. *Fin de Siecle.* That *Fin* would be finned sounds right! But they are fins with a twist. And eyes with a twist, too. The wandering eye has a real champion in the eye of the halibut, and, as we shall see, in this sole Sole's soul ... who's feeling only so-so, tanked and all.

So ... Jim is at last on the schooner of his halibut dreams, but Life has in the meantime offered him a way to make a living not killing, and he has taken the bait. Still, he shares his halibut dreams with Captain John, owner/builder of the schooner, *Mycia*, and his wife and first mate, Melinda. Even though he knows that catching or killing halibut is no longer his destiny, Jim is wondering what his present has to do with all those past halibut dreams? He's about to find out.

Read all about it! The cross-eyed creature from four trillion angstroms* meets a rodeo roper!

We begin on the morning of June twenty-fifth, 2004, when the *Mycia* gang sails into Meyer's Chuck, British Columbia, a deep and quiet bay on Canada's Inland Passage. We tie up alongside the fishing boat *Hula Girl*, captained by Morgan with wife Caroline, Maui friends who winter in Hawaii and fish in Alaska's stunning summers.

Morgan can't wait to tell us a tale of an outrageously athletic halibut. It goes that when bringing up their catch of black cod from two hundred fathoms this fish has followed it up and jumped aboard the boat! All thirty pounds of him! And he is swimming in the boat's live bait tank right now! They have never seen this happen, and Zantar, the Halibut Seeker, (a.k.a. Jim) has arrived alongside. What could be the connection?

Only one tried and true method to find out: interview the halibut. The plot thickens, but will this halibut thicken the soup? James the Just won't just kill a fish, as he would as a child. So the dory-schooner-halibut-fishing fantasy has verily escaped him. Leapt out of his mental net, and he is left wondering, what remains?

* four trillion angstroms = 200 fathoms = 1,200 feet

That the very boat they've tied along side has a *live volunteer halibut* in their fish tank? The first? Ever? No hook? From twelve hundred feet below? Jumped into the boat? Hello! Destiny calling? For sure! Jim schedules an interview.

Efforts are made to encircle the Halibut's tail with a line by an Iranian deckhand named Younis, but to no avail. Jim gathers his mar-kit* forces gear (mask, snorkel, and Speedos™) and plunges into the icy halibut-inhabited tank for the interview.

Big breath. Dive!

Anxious minutes pass for the watchers. Children stand peering into the tank, having lost sight of their grandpa. Younis has not expected a long-breath-hold dolphin diver, and he's ready to go in to save Jim! All wait in heart-pounding silence.

> *Below the surface, I disappear and follow Hal to the end of the tank. Then, whispering to me, Hal introduces the concept of his release as opposed to a human feast.*
>
> *Sending a telepathic reply, I counter, "Good point, but what's in it for us? Why should we, especially our domestic angels, Melinda and Caroline, let*

---

* mar-kit (kit for the sea) = market forces, being the predominant influences in Western economies.

dinner for thirty just flip and slip away? Why fish if you don't keep your catch?"

Hal recognizes this as a very good point, as he himself spent many years as a carnivore before recognizing the spiritual peace granted vegetarians. He further suggests that the hunter/gladiator men might give him a thumbs up for his timely arrival for an interview*–for God's sake, leaping into the Boat! However, he gets that a female feeding her family is a toughie to go up against.*

So there must be a sign. Something Super Flukish and Cosmical.

I look deeply into his twisted eyes ... which twists my brain strangely ... POP! Some mental thing is feeling back in alignment after being out for years! Whew!

My antique college-level mind lights up and the thoughts stampede off. Something like this: I think ... or am being thought ... or am hearing a whisper in my mind ... that eyes on either side of the head are prey *eyes: eyes on the same side–like ours up front–are* predator *eyes: Biology 101! The halibut's eyes started as those of a* prey*, and by one eye twisting 'round in their maturation to the other side, became those of a* predator*. And a very laid back one at that, resting on the bottom, striking upward: Psychology 101 and War Games 101.*

And then, being able to look into their own eyes ignites consciousness: seeing seeing. Fractal reflectivity embodied: Cybernetics 101!

Humans were prey for millennia and having vanquished all their predators ... but themselves ... are adjusting to being predators, and vanquishing themselves: Paleo-Anthropology 101!

My mind drifts into mathematical realms: I wonder about the Mobius strip: it went from two sides to one. Is this maturing predatoriness, like the halibut? Giving up prey status? My United Species one-sided Flag ... maturing predation, when its whole goal is promoting peace??? Mathematical Biology and Sociobiology 101! Whoa! I'll think about it later.

My long breath holding skills are being tested, and there is more halibut whispering to endure and decode. And here I thought I was the whisper-or, but now I'm the whisper-ee, and being solicited as a halibut masseur and rodeo roper! I'm feeling more professional already. At last, some New Age perks! Hundred bucks an hour by Tuesday! I'll breathe later!

I let Hal sniff and view the rope I've brought with the loop on the end, push a loop through that loop and slip it gently over Hal's tail. I break the surface and suck in a huge breath to cheers and sighs of relief from the admiring crowd.

This isn't at all like shooting fish in a barrel! Everybody knows it. Something really professional going on. They step back and give me room. I cinch up the noose, lift Hal out of the tank, give him a brief lower back massage and an unexpected quick jerk, get a photo, and put him back in the fish tank, tail noose tight.

"Ah," he whispers somewhere in the back of my mind, "I got some release there." I wonder personally if he is not implanting the idea of *his* release with this suggestion. Like, a little release is good, and a lot is better.

So I talk to the female cooks, Caroline and Melinda. Melinda demurs: it's Caroline's catch.

"No Way Jose! Thirty pounds of meat ... a hundred bucks at Safeway! You *are* kidding, aren't you?" Caroline is having a hard time with the results of my interview with a "human whispering" halibut. Even if it *is* a volunteer! Not even hooked! We didn't catch it: it caught us, *etc.*

"No!" Caroline explains. "Blah, blah, blah. Dream on, dreamer," *etc.* Round one goes to Caroline!

Round two. Searching for a sign, something undeniably mysterious (or else something baked with plenty of tartar sauce, which?), I feel myself weakening: "*lots* of tartar sauce?" I ask, mouth watering.

Of a sudden, I'm magnetically drawn back to the tank.

Hal is there ... free! Out of the loop and swimming on the surface!

I call Caroline to witness Hal's sublime freedom. And I review for her the old story about the rock that was rolled away from Christ's burial tomb at Golgotha. The parallels are undeniable! She saw the loop I tied, but Hal is out! "Shall we re-crucify Christ?" I suggest.

She looks at me with sort of a fishy eye, a little like Hal's, and smiles a really beautiful smile after I tell her Hal is actually Halley, a pregnant female-wise-being, Mary Magdalene perhaps, and very close to delivery.

So Caroline rolls her eyes and says, "Ooo-kay, let her go. I guess she's a *non-profit* prophetess."

With a few loud yells the whole gang assembles. Younis gets the loop back over the tail and lifts the fish out of the tank, as cameras flasho, recording joint Iranian/American cooperation complete with victory signs! Grandkids come in for a close eye-to-eye with Halley before her release. Hearty goodbyes and over the side–splasho!

Hal did two vertical re-orientation revolutions and one flat out skeedaddle. Eddie* and Hal wud go. And *went!* *Hallelujah!*

---

* Eddie (Edward Ryon Makuhanai) Aikau (1946-1978) – legendary surfer and lifeguard who risked his life to save many and lost his own going to save the *Hokule'a*.

"Inaction may be the biggest form of action."

– Governor Jerry Brown

Blackwater

Blackwater, a.k.a. Xe, LLC = Re-Bilderbergers

Who hasn't read about Blackwater's outrageous cruelties and financial thievery? Google it and cry!

Question: What's happened to America?

Answer: The Re-Bilderberger's new answer: If it doesn't need re-building, bomb it ... so it does! Profits forever!

Re-Bilderberger's CREDO:
"A cathedral is just a cathedral until
Someone envisions it as a pile of rocks!"

All this outrageousness! The Re-Builderbergers had lucrative government contracts for re-building, but they found it more profitable to stay in the destruction phase, rather than the re-building phase. Now, Blackwater, LLC has even bought out Backwater [Guns] LLC that had bought up all the still operational bazookas, planes, and aircraft carriers from WW II. This is what President Eisenhower warned us against –the "military-industrial complex". Well, they can just call it a "Postmodern Deconstruction" phase, to have the humanities department of every university on their side. For now, the pseudo-Re-Builderbergers postmodern deconstructioners are practicing, like doctors. Just look around. Practice makes perfect!

And wouldn't you know, Blackwater LLC has changed their name to Xe, L.L.C. to avoid the bad association with their name, "Blackwater." Its founder says that someone, for political reasons, threw him under the bus, so he was forced to resign and reduce his ownership and other perks. Says he wants to become a high school teacher!?!

MORE LATE BREAKING NEWS:
    Hey Slackers, we missed it again!
    What?
    Something for nothing!
    Let's do a show, okay?

COMING SOON-er or later!

THE RETURN OF THE SLACKERS
(Directed by Jim's slacker cat Jewels)

Jewels had noted that not only was his bowl out of water, but that Slackers should have their own water. Every new-age group has their own favorite brand of bottled water. Jim, his slacker owner, should have his own brand of water to share with Jewels, as well as that burger he's been building …!

At last, water for slackers! "SLACKWATER"™ (Unlike BLACKWATER, which has left a stinking string of bullet-riddled corpses in its wake.)

THE SLACKWATER™ CREDO:
"We Don't Do Anything,
So No One Gets Hurt."

We're not saying SLACKWATER™ ain't black backwater.
We're just saying, "IF IT'S MOVIN'…
IT AIN'T US!"

Note: Since this writing, the owner of Xe, LLC has retired from teaching and received a private contract to guard Saudi Arabia's leaders for 1.7 billion dollars.

"Two roads diverged ... and I
... took the road less traveled by,
And that has made all the difference.
— Robert Frost

Archer and Lockyer

The last time I was in my hometown of Long Beach, California, I went by my *alma mater*, Long Beach State College (LBSC). Visits to the mainland have been infrequent since coming to Maui, so I wanted to invest this time in connecting with old memories. Years before, I'd earned a couple of degrees from State, but I found myself searching out what suddenly mattered most to me, finding the old rowing club on the Marine Stadium. I'd crewed in '58: remembering those early morning workouts in our eight-man shell swiftly skimming over quiet water now brought me here.

But here I found *not* the little open shed that had housed the long shells and one-man sculls–with the faucet and hose to rinse off with–but lo' and behold, the Pete Archer Rowing Center, a new and exquisitely equipped facility on a par with any East Coast crewing association's. Wow! Besides a full-on gym, locker rooms for boys *and* girls, and stacks of racks of rowing shells, there were walls lined with photos dating back to way before my time.

There he was! My old coach, Pete Archer himself, older than I'd remembered him, but beaming that unmistakable smile at the camera. And there was my first boss, Bill Lockyer, sitting in a scull on the water at the Marine Stadium, looking young and ready for the '32 Olympics. I'd worked in Bill's market as a kid, and later he'd guided me to the boat of my dreams: a varnished spruce lapstrake double-ender with sliding seats and oar extensions for two.

These were fond memories of now fabled guys, men of distinction, memories to savor. Photos of crew teams from down the years were displayed, but I didn't see any photos of my team from 1958, which was, incidentally, LBSC's first rowing team. Lucky I had the very picture and sent a copy to the Center to add to this history of rowing.

Looking back, I was stroke on the team, but they moved me back a position because I broke too many oars. Set too fierce a pace. Some oars might have been there since the Olympics, so I may have just been clearing out the dead wood. But in the picture I'm the guy on the right, so you can see how it might have happened: oars took one look and just gave up. (See photo F, page 131.)

I first met Pete Archer when he was the swimming coach at my high school, and there he was at LBSC, still coaching swimming. So, when I was in my last year working toward my Bachelor of Science I figured I could take time out to break a few school records–with this record string of broken oars and all. I scheduled a try-out with swim Coach Pete to impress him.

I had a personal history of breaking school athletic records, so it seems my confidence was well-founded. After having set Jefferson Junior High School records in the ninth grade in football throwing fifty-five yards and running a 5.9-second fifty-yard and 10.5-second hundred-yard dash, I came to high school with promise. My beautiful older sister, who happened to be a spirited cheerleader at Wilson High, made sure Jim Lineberger, the football coach, heard of me. Hearing tales of a big strong freshman coming his way, he contacted me in the summer before school started. On the beach he saw my speed and my impossibly long football throws and catches and made me a fullback! I memorized my fullback position moves, and on the first scrimmage charged through a hole that wasn't there ... but two teammates were. After that first bone-breaking play I quit! Too much damage! With Coach Jim yelling at me to come back, I walked over to Coach Pete Archer's swim team. But after one day I couldn't take the echoing noise and chlorine of the indoor pool, and I quit in favor of my own solo open-ocean rowing and diving.

I kept a rowboat on the roof of my car throughout college. I'd row out to the end of the Long Beach breakwater, put on my mask and fins, dive fifty feet for scallops, and drift towards home studying for exams alone at sea lying in the bottom of my rocking boat ... and later a great scallop dinner. What a Life! To be free on the open sea rocking in your old-time classic lapstrake boat and challenging your mind to dive deeper!

I have to admit, drifting had been a way of life ever since I was about twelve when my dad dropped me off at Point Fermin with a huge truck tire inner tube that had a piece of plywood lashed over the hole and a good book to read– wouldn't you know, *Huckleberry Finn.* I drifted across Long Beach Harbor–not so busy then–and down the entire bay ending up at the jetty near Seal Beach. Each time Dad would show up in his '35 Ford, we'd lash my rig on top, and home we'd go.

But here I was back again with Coach Pete Archer at LBSC seven years after deserting high school team sports. My friend Bill Price, who had been a champion on the swim team for six years, was with me. And I was about to catch up! What's six years of practice? I asked Pete what he thought after witnessing a few of my lightning-speed churning laps.

No comment.

I looked at Pete.

Quiet. Very quiet.

"Yes?" I asked hopefully.

"Ahem … well … you could say (trying not to smirk), you might say that you look like a prehistoric dinosaur taking his early morning bath!" Then he flashed me that smile of his.

Fifty years have passed, and I'm known for free diving to one hundred feet, was called the "dolphin man" on Maui for years, and I'm noted in books on dolphins. In *Call Of The Dolphins,* I'm chapter twenty: "Living the Dolphin Lifestyle." Either I improved my swimming style from Archer's coaching, or dolphins appreciate my primitive form. Maybe both.

But getting to the dolphins and rowing channels started with that lovely lapstrake double-ender that Bill Lockyer found for me. In that boat I studied for high school and college exams, spent summers exploring the Catalina coast with my buddy Ben, romanced my beautiful young wife, and set solo and tandem rowing records to Catalina Island. In the summer of '68 I acquired another favorite rowboat, a Newport Coast Guard cutter lifeboat with a beautiful wine-glass stern.

Eventually I shipped both boats, my mother's grand piano, and five hundred feet of rope to Maui. In an attempt to save my wooden boats from being devoured by hungry tropical pests and mold, Craig Mathison (another Wilson High boy) successfully turned one of the wooden hulls into fiberglass. The Lockyer boat, through no fault of Craig's, stuck in the mold. I guess it was destined to be one with mold no matter how hard we tried to save her.

Fortunately, the fiberglass version of the Coast Guard lifeboat, extended by two feet, slipped out of the mold and into the sea. It has afforded me a hundred thousand different strokes with many different folks down coasts and across other channels between Maui, Lanai, and Molokai for the past thirty-five years. After a recent paint job, a new set of rails, oarlocks, and oars, that surviving lifeboat has been re-launched and christened *Row-mance,* describing what it has been for me, and as an allusion to Don Quixote's trusty steed, named "Rocinante" [rohw-sin-aun-te]. The boat played a part in the film *Get a Job,* Maui's own "home" movie. And now my grandkids are carrying on the tradition with me, rowing and diving in quiet coves on sunny mornings. What a Life!

Interspecies nuzzling

"We can't become what we need to be by remaining what we are."

– Oprah Winfrey

Advertisement

United Species
US

Creating enlarged allegiances and alliances

If you are a member of a Species ... Welcome!

This website is for you!

Our intention is an extension of allegiance to the Whole!

To the whole Cosmos that birthed you–
Bio-Cosmic-Centrism!

The whole Cosmos and its beings,

Which is known to include us and US–United Species.

Feeling constrained by anthropomorphic or political limitations ... United States ... United Nations? Breakout! Come on over to United Species!

To join the United Species (US)

1) Go to **www.savingthecosmostiltuesday.com**

2) Fill out the Entry Form with

  a) Your Kingdom, phylum, class, order, family, genus, species;

  b) Your address–Galaxy, star, planet, nation, state, city, mailing & street address, and pod;

3) Click on "Join."

4) Print out your free numbered membership certificate in PDF.

Go to www.savingthecosmostiltuesday.com for your Passport to the Universe!

The United Species requires a flag that will be created in the United Species Underwater Parade Uniting Civilizations (USUPUC).

1) The parade will involve a deep-water breath-hold diver from each of the Earth's 195 nations.

2) Each diver will wear a cape that has the flag of their nation on one side and the animal of their nation on the other.

3) Wearing their capes, the divers will create the underwater parade by diving in a spiral formation down to sixty feet under water and then swimming back up to the surface through the descending divers, creating a double helix, the

shape of DNA common to all species, in a scale of ten billion to one.

4) As the divers begin their ascent, they will each remove their cape and join it to the others, eventually forming one large United Species Flag.

5) Attached to rings and wires, the flag will form a wedding ring that encircles the finger-like column of spiraling divers.

A new marriage! With a new twist! We then give the flag a half twist, and it becomes a Mobius flag with countries' flags and animals on the same side. A flag of flags! At last! A Flag complex enough for these complex times!

The history of evolution is that of growing towards greater complexity.

Get with the FLOW! A new flag for a new State of Mind ...

United Species Earth

Be of USE* ... Join Today!
www.savingthecosmostiltuesday.com

* Tell us on your application if you want to be a part of creating the USUPUC flag.

(say, "Us up, you see?")

"Now I see the secret of the making of the best persons. It is to grow in the open air and eat and sleep with the Earth."
— Walt Whitman

Life in the Trees

Ours is the thrill of our *doing* becoming our *being*:
We live in our gardens ...

Wake to bird songs in the rustling trees,
Morning Jacuzzi in chiseled rock pools in clear rapid stream.
Thirty foot cliff dive wake-up begins mile swim
In deep, wide pool.

Meditate in massive cave ...
Pool shimmers in morning sun
Throwing waves of rippling light
Onto high cave dome.

Gushing spring in crevice of cliff keeps pool full, clear.
Sit on gravel beach and skip stones across pool
To where roots of banyan cling to towering cliff face;
Skip ... skip ... skip ... click-splash!

Climb up rooted path hand over hand out to steep edge,
Toes grip rock, spine skyward, soaking in warmth of sun:
Breathe deep from center of earth,
Chest high. Dive again outward into sky.

Enter clear pool clean, underwater flip, emerge in
    butterfly stroke.
Long languid rope-swing beckons for one last leap,
Grab on and swing ... swing ... swing ... flip-splash!
Swim to easy exit at underwater stone steps.

Hike up steep path through colorful, fragrant jungle,
Pause to gaze deep into hanging orchids,
Push aside vines to see sweetheart coming to greet.
Feed each other morning nasturtiums covered in
    rainbow dew.

Together, gather abundant fruits, always enough to share:
Banana, lilikoi, coconut, guava, pungent Surinam cherry;
Bring to friends this gathered feast of ripe fruit and laughter
    rife with ease.

life in the trees

Sing our prayers* of thanks for plants and another
    beautiful day.
Weed twenty-one bed garden** to start new compost pile.
Harvest lettuce, carrots, beets, and herbs for splendid
    noontime salad.
Rake fresh leaves onto outdoor kitchen floor, ready for
    guests.
Workday done by nine.

Open coconut after drinking its milk from papaya stem
    straw,
Pop out white spoon-meat with shell edge into mouth;
Slip into hammock and rock with coco in the breeze.
Enjoy long view of four waves peeling off the point.

Lovebirds sing and cling to bamboo tree-house branch.
Bearing red ginger and pink butterfly
To my red-flowered grass-skirted bare-breasted beauty,
Greeted with kisses and fondest hellos.

---

* "Blessings on the blossom, blessings on the root, blessings on the leaves and stems, blessings on the fruit." 4 part round (Waldorf)

** John Jevons' Biodynamic mini-farm to ensure sustainable global survival in the 21st century: twenty-one 5'x20' beds equaling 2,100 square feet of arable land/person on Earth.

It's *your* time, dear reader,

To share sky blue pillows and pink sheets,

Curl up with your cat in your bamboo-grass-shack

With your blessed sweetheart treehouse love,

And let the blue stars fall.

Acknowledgments

Aloha and *mahalo* to the many organizations that have arisen in defense of Nature, and especially to the individuals and groups who have supported me in my global eco-adventures: Greenpeace via John Perry's "Save the Whales Now;" Christine Stevens' Animal Welfare Institute; Joan Mac Intyre's "Project Jonah;" Tatman Foundation, which trusted me with the sailing research vessel, "The Tutunui;" and Zaca Lake's "whale woman," who traded me a lakeside cabin, wherein Robert Louis Stevenson once wrote, for my daily sunset piano concert.

And acknowledgments to the last, lost tribe of two hundred pre-modern Jivaro Indians of Colombia … who need all the help they can get. Say I'm a *post*-modern Jivaro, a cartoon Tarzan who has eco-capered through modernity, and taken his chances returning to Nature, in hopes of keeping that distance our civilization requires for an honest assessment of its current direction. At last, I'm the lost, lone scout reporting in.

And then there's that shameless Macho-Stallions Club to thank: Roy Smith, Rico Bailey, Billy Wittman, Robert Malerba, and Andy Ridinger for their brilliant one-liners that always throw new light on Man's condition, foregoing serious, uncomfortable truth with smiling, devastating humor about our dubious chances for long-term survival. And *mahalo* to Brian Wittman, parent *extraordinaire,* and his son, Makila, for being there when I needed them. And an everlasting *mahalo* to Todd Swan, videographer of an era, for his archiving our unique lives. And more thanks to Paul Forrest, comrade-in-arms in this search for meaning we all pursue.

I must add to this list of appreciations *couples* who have made their impact on my writing, especially of this book: to John and Louise Severson–John my buddy, everlasting cohort, and creative midwife; and Louise, his artful and steadfast partner–thank you. Another couple, Alizé de Rosnay and Nathan Howe, have also honored me by supporting my place in Maui's hippy history. Alizé's father, Baron Arnaud de Rosnay, windsurfed the straits of the world to effect reconciliation between countries alienated by political differences. My undying appreciation to him! And thanks to schooner builders, Captain John and Melinda Maher, who embraced the Maui family and are cherished by many.

These forty-two chapters–vignettes gleaned from what has been a huge forty-two years-long writing project–wouldn't be in your hands without the support of three very special women in my life. But first of all, loving thanks to *all* the women in my life–all of them wise women, athletes, and thinkers whom I've had the privilege of knowing: Elizabeth, my loving mother; Jo Ann, my beautiful sister; Mary Alice, my generous mother-in-law; Shakeena, my exquisite granddaughter; Shelley and her daughter, Kiana, both my oh-so-talented, lovely nieces; Nancy; O'Brien; Yosha; Danya; Lasensua; D.B.; Christina; Suzanie; Fiddle Mary; Joana; Debbie; Carla; Alicia; Natalie; Lana; Maureen; Starheart; Patricia; Nina; Katrina; Lili; Radiance; Sunshine; Marianna; Lucy-in-the-Sky; Selena; young Viva; and Shell–thanks to all for putting up with my wild ways. And there have been some other feminine Angels along the way: Diane Firestone, Advaita Bach, Lucy Williams, and Cynthia Matzke. Mahalo for seeing me through.

So now–drumroll, please–*mahalo nui loa* to those three lovely loving women who were determined to see this book–the prequel to the *magnum opus*–launched: my former and only wife, Diana Dahl; my daughter, Megan Powers; and my friend, Barbara Wood. Barbara–with her knowledge of books and publishing, her design sense, and her enthusiasm for my writing–has been an invaluable help from the beginning. Thank you.

I must also thank more friends and family, some whose names appear in these pages, and others who have helped shape my output through the years: John Manners, my first Hawaiian benefactor; Ben Hawkins, my Catalina buddy; Ty and Jack Ewing: John Perry, artist activist; Greg Kaufman and all the Whale Nuts; Craig Mathison; Daniel McCulloch; Andrew Annenberg; William "Tab" Ballantine; "Aeternitas;" Kim Kindersly; Napier Martin; Steve Corrick; Lou de Bourbon; Dave Sachs; Jamie Waits; Rick Bickford, Kevin Block; Dustin Hengel; Adam Sisolak; Mark Gregg; Richard Abdullah; Nick Fornier, Steve Spencer; Peter Kraft; Daniel Cohen; Michael Dattola; Nahiku; and Jackie Tavares.

Finally, thanks to Zen Powers, my grandson, for loving to write poetry; to my dad, Joe, and my son, Gannon; to Max Powers, soil builder and solid dad; to Jacques Mayol and Les Dahl, inspirational watermen both; and Richard Kirsch, John Tullius, and Robert Loomis of Random House, for recognizing my take on things as worth honoring.

"Let the blue stars fall."
— Jim Loomis

Afterword

My appreciation goes to the awakening citizens young and old of the Occupy Movement who are speaking truth to power and to those children of the 1% who will listen and make real change for a better world.

Our Products

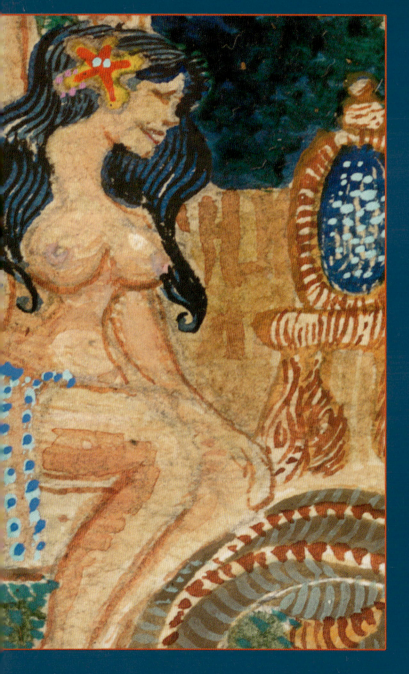

The Book
Digital Book
Art Prints
T-shirts
Aquabet Font
(and more!)

*Join us!
Become a
member of
"United Species"*

savingthecosmostiltuesday.com